Together in Hope

Proclaiming God's Justice Living God's Love

Edited by Adrian Alker

On behalf of the
Inclusive Church Network

The logo and the subtitle on the front of this book are those of the Inclusive Church Network, a partnership of organisations first brought together in preparation for the 2008 Lambeth Conference.

St Marks CRC Press Sheffield

Printed by Pickard Communication, Sheffield, UK

Contents

Better Together

Adrian Alker is vicar of St Mark's Church, Broomhill, Sheffield

My working life began in Liverpool and it was in that city's imposing Anglican cathedral some years later that I was ordained as a priest in the Church of England. Church life and attendance was buoyant in the north west during those years of the 1970's but a significant blot on the landscape was the continuing distrust and, in the case of Northern Ireland, open hostility, between some in the Roman Catholic and Protestant communities. That lack of tolerance and understanding between different Christian denominations was to energise the efforts of many church leaders to work closer together for the sake of the gospel of Jesus Christ. Liverpool's Hope Street connects the Anglican and Roman Catholic cathedrals and their respective bishops David Sheppard and Archbishop Derek Warlock worked tirelessly side by side as Christian leaders and close friends. Their example of collaboration, their shared vision of how the Christian faith compels us to work for a world of peace and justice for all people, inspired many of us in those years and since.

Today, in this twenty-first century, the churches face different challenges. In the United Kingdom there has been a well-chronicled decline in churchgoing, while at the same time a persistent interest in religion and spirituality. For Anglicans dissension over matters of sexuality and gender seem to absorb much energy as the Lambeth Conference gathers again. The ecumenical endeavours of previous generations seem less able now to cope with a sharper polarisation between conservative and more progressive voices. These seem to be sharper, more polemical times. Religious fundamentalism, allied to violence, dominates much of the public discourse on matters of faith. In the face of this what hope is there for people of faith to work together for the sake of God's world? There are two central convictions which have driven me to produce this small book, both born out of my thirty years experience as a parish priest. First of all I am convinced that most people both in our churches and those on the edge desire to see more working together, more collaboration and less confrontation between various groups and factions, claiming to know and speak 'the truth'. Secondly we should not underestimate the desire of many people for a truly fresh expression of what it means to be people of faith today. At times there seems to be a conspiracy of silence between Christian ministers and congregations when it comes to radical thinking, with clergy somewhat reluctant to 'upset' their members by too much critical thinking whilst those very members may be yearning for more solid food! We really do need to 'grow up into Christ' (Ephesians 4. 15). This book and its contents is offered then in this spirit.

What do we hope for?

This book is the outcome of a number of meetings between various organisations wishing to share their vision for the Christian faith and the Church. Over the past two years I have had the pleasure of meeting with key people in many different organisations-some could be described as pressure groups, some have very focussed concerns, some groups represent particular Christian denominations, some have been founded to enable people to reflect theologically, some are concerned with prayer, some with issues of global justice. The centre pages of this book are a kind of directory, giving details of the work of many such organisations (but by no means all) and encouraging the reader to follow up whatever might be of interest.

Through the ten short chapters of this book the reader is presented with a landscape of hope as the authors share their insights and convictions about God and the Kingdom, about Jesus, the Bible, about the nature of the Church, about those on the margins of society. In 2008 an initiative was launched called Hope08. What are we hoping for? Throughout this book runs the firm belief that nothing less than a radical revisioning of Christianity will be necessary to face the challenges of the twenty-first century. A truly fresh expression of what it means to be Christian, and of how the Church can be true to this vision, has little to do with cosmetic changes or management-speak.

Rather it is offering to those in the churches and those without, an intelligent, open hearted and convincing way forward, leading to a rich experience of the inclusive and demanding love of God seen in Jesus. These chapters therefore are meant to stimulate thought and discussion, and hence the questions for reflection at the end of each chapter. I hope therefore the book may be an aid for group discussion.

This book is also a modest attempt to offer some resources to those who see faith and Church as a journey of discovery, of learning, of gaining insights from one another. Bishop Jack Spong has often said that he wishes that churches could be places where people are encouraged to ask the questions and not just be given answers. In living the questions we so often open our hearts and minds to a greater Wisdom. Suggestions for further reading accompany each chapter and the final pages offer the reader some further resources.

"Proclaiming God's Justice, Living God's Love"

The above phrase has been chosen by the group of organisations who have supported the publication of this book. I am deeply grateful to the authors who have, in their different ways, enlarged upon this theme. Steven Shakespeare invites us first of all to consider what we mean by the word God and how our experiences can help shape that understanding. Steven and Hugh Rayment-Pickard expand this thinking in their splendid book, *The Inclusive God*.

Two eminent North American scholars follow. Marcus Borg invites us to consider how Jesus reveals this God to us, and Dominic Crossan compares and contrasts the Kingdom programme of Jesus with the teaching of John the Baptiser. Marcus Borg and Dominic Crossan exemplify how the fruits of the study of the historical Jesus, not least from the Jesus Seminar school in the USA, have helped to revise our understanding of the significance of Jesus and his message for Christian faith.

Keith Ward, in addition to the many other books and articles which he has written, has more recently defended the use of the bible against the onslaught of literalists, and reminds us of its central importance to Christian faith, and how the bible must be read intelligently.

A number of organisations and networks aim to help people on their journey of faith. Hugh Dawes and Jill Sandham, working out of the Progressive Christianity Network (PCN Britain), challenge us in chapter five, to recapture that hopeful way of being church where each member carries the stamp and mark of Jesus. Jonathan Clatworthy invites us, as does the Modern Churchpeople's Union, of which he is General Secretary, to embrace the challenges of the modern world. Rather than see modernity with its scientific and technological advances as the natural enemy of faith, we are invited to discern what is of God's goodness and purpose (and what is not) in such progress.

Two chapters, from Christina Rees and Clare Herbert, invite the reader to consider how being 'in Christ' invites full participation in the household of God for women, standing equally alongside men, and for gay and lesbian people living out their Christian vocation in company with straight people.

Lest we fail to lift up our eyes and see the suffering of so many in God's world, Paula Clifford, the Head of Theology at Christian Aid, reminds us that the hope of the poorest people in the world lies in how their suffering must become our suffering and our response.

This landscape of the proclamation of God's justice and love ends appropriately in Jim Cotter's reflection on how our worship and our prayers express that hope within us. Such worship and the thoughtful use of language play a crucial role in offering to those who come into our church communities a freshly inspiring approach to the God who calls us to work together in hope and in love.

Sheffield

I began this introduction on a personal note, referring to the former Bishop of Liverpool, David Sheppard. We all need our exemplars of faith, those saints of God whom we encounter on the road. David Sheppard and Grace his wife were two such people in their work together for the people of that diocese and city. In the last twenty years, the saints of God for me have been the people at St Mark's Church in Broomhill in Sheffield with whom it has been a joy for me to rediscover a faith fit for this new millennium. Together we have dared to risk asking those big questions, dared to open up our doubts and fears, dared to question much dogmatic teaching. However this has not been a negative or vacuous exercise, which empties a church and robs Christianity of its vitality. Rather such 'honest to God' exploration not only has a time-honoured place in Christian discipleship, but also has reinvigorated the church community and made it a place of open heartedness. In the establishment of the Centre for Radical Christianity (St Mark's CRC) we have welcomed many scholars and church people, and nearly all of the contributors to this book have been our guests at St Mark's. It is therefore with a profound sense of gratitude that I thank them and all the people of St Mark's for their companionship and their love.

This book is published under the auspices of St Mark's CRC. I am grateful for its financial and administrative help. Thanks are also due to the organisations in the Inclusive Church Network and to the Open Theology Trust who have part-funded this venture. My work in pulling together this book has been made easier by the help of Dr Chris Knight and the excellent staff of Pickard Communication in Sheffield.

Two further things need to be said. This book as a whole expresses one particular way of seeing and commending the Christian life and faith. For many this will not be their way. Although representative of a collaboration between certain groups, which might be called open, liberal, progressive, inclusive (choose your term), I do not intend this book to be polemic. It is offered as a positive description of the Christian hope as many of us see it. Furthermore it does not presume that the various organisations listed in the directory all agree on everything theological! The views expressed in the chapters are those of their authors. The directory entries come from each group without any editing. For the rest of the book I take responsibility.

Finally I am conscious of the book's limitations and omissions. It was never intended to be a book on Christian doctrine, there are many of those and many people far better qualified to write them. However I sincerely hope that in this year of Hope08 this book will be a stimulus to thought and action and an example of how together we can be people of hope in the world today.

Adrian Alker
Broomhill, Sheffield
June 2008

The God of Hope – the God Difference

Steven Shakespeare is the Anglican chaplain at Liverpool Hope University.

'Not only is there no God, but try getting a plumber on weekends'.

Woody Allen's quip sums up a common modern attitude to God, shared by believers and nonbelievers alike. In a world that seems to run on its own laws, God only needs to be brought in when the plumbing breaks down. When things go wrong, when we can't explain them, the Great Fixer is called.

Some still have confidence in this idea of God, intervening in our world and our personal lives directly to sort things out. God has the plan, and we just need his expertise to set us on track.

Others, both inside and outside the churches, are not so sure. If God is a Great Fixer, why is it that so much still seems to be wrong with the world? Why are his representatives so obviously human and imperfect? Is he a divine Cowboy, someone who fails to inspire confidence and faith?

In the wake of these questions, it's perhaps not surprising that many find no need to believe in such a being. God is either not up to the job, or else completely unnecessary. The world might be in a mess, but it is naïve to think that a divine hand can reach in from the outside to set it right. Better to focus on what we as human beings can do, and let science and practical wisdom be our guides.

I understand this point of view. This God doesn't work, any more than the untraceable plumber. But I will argue that this is not the last word on the matter. This idea of God is a very narrow one. It is in fact an idol: a small, lifeless thing we have created to soothe our fears or satisfy our needs. When it is found wanting, the risk is that we throw it out, never suspecting that there might be another truth.

I want to affirm a richer vision of God, one that avoids becoming a pale and irrelevant reflection of our own hang-ups. It is a vision which draws upon the living witness of the Bible and what Christians have taught, prayed and lived down the centuries. But God is not the possession of any one group, or language. God is not a dead source of power for a self-appointed elect.

No, this God makes a difference. You might say God makes all the difference in the world.

God in relationship

The Christian teaching of the Trinity—that God is Father, Son and Holy Spirit—might not seem a very promising place to start. The idea that there is one God, but three 'persons' sounds like a conundrum dreamt up by theologians—complicated, confusing and distant from real life.

In fact, the teaching came about because Christians were trying to do justice to their very real, life-changing *experience* of God. They believed in God, the source of all life, being and beauty. But they believed in a new way because their life had been touched by Jesus, and they came to see him as the image and revelation of God's own character. Jesus was God's Word, made flesh. The ultimate truth, made personal. And, finally, Christians experienced an outpouring of God's presence through the Holy Spirit. The Spirit was wild and free, it guided and drove them, it comforted and confirmed their faith, it made them dream new dreams. It broke down barriers between people.

Christians experience a God of relationships, a God who is the giving and receiving of love. Not a lonely, detached being, ruling from above, but light, cloud, music, breath, fire, compassion, love. This is what the well-worn phrase 'God is love' means. God is never solitary, never fragmented.

Faith means realising that we are invited into that relationship of love. Because God is love, we are accepted. We do not compete for love, there are no favourites. God wants full, abundant life for us all.

This is a radical message. In a world dominated by hierarchies of rich and poor, men and women, white and black, north and south, straight and gay, faith in God affirms a love which undercuts them all. At their best, our scriptures bear witness to this love. They should not be turned into a substitute for the dynamic event of God's reaching out to us. At their best, our churches extend love's invitation. They should never claim to control and police it.

The teaching of the Trinity is important, because it offers us a vision of a living God. A living God always escapes the grasp of our concepts and images. No one name can label God and leave nothing more to be said. So there is a tremendous freshness and openness about this God, who can be encountered in many ways, under many names.

The event of love opens out to us in unexpected experiences, and finds its voice in those who have been silenced or excluded. It calls for a different kind of community, a community of welcome, hospitality and inclusion in a world (and a church) where rigid barriers of identity, fear and suspicion too often rule our lives.

Christians affirm that God cannot be reduced to being a part of the world, a force we can contain or comprehend. But neither is the God of relationships set apart from the world. God is met in and through otherness, the people and creatures, the places and experiences which open us to new possibilities, responsibilities and invitations.

This is the context in which it makes sense to talk of another great teaching of Christian faith: creation.

Creation

As the scientific world view took root in the eighteenth century, its power of observation and experiment re-shaped the medieval cosmos. In place of a fixed world which pointed beyond itself to God, who gave it movement and purpose, scientists proposed something very different. First, a world of mechanical laws, which needed no supernatural hand to keep it going or explain it, and which aimed at no goal beyond itself. Secondly, a view of life which evolved, adapted and mutated through huge stretches of time, obeying laws of survival which had little to do with morality or providence.

Nowadays, science has moved a great deal from a crude mechanical view of natural laws, but for many it still leaves little room for God. Supernatural truths are pushed out to the margins, or confined to people's private beliefs. If they emerge in public in any assertive way, it is often in the guise of fundamentalism, whose anti-modern, anti-science stance and exclusive claims seem irrational and dangerous. For some critics of religion, this only confirms that God is a superstitious delusion.

What future then for belief in God? One thing is clear. A faith which simply sets itself in opposition to science is not truly critical or liberating. It becomes a negative image of what it tries to reject, claiming absolute pseudo-scientific certainty for its dogmas. And it misses the intricacy, beauty and connectedness that science reveals about our world.

Rather than pitting God against science, or trying to squeeze God into the gaps in our knowledge, we need to ask ourselves where the questions of meaning and value really come to life for us. Whatever theory we adopt about the beginning of the cosmos, the origins of life or human evolution, those questions remain.

Believing in creation is not an irrational claim that the world was made in six days a few thousand years ago. It is a way of keeping alive our sense that life matters, that it cannot simply be reduced to the collisions of particles and chemical reactions without something being lost. Even scientific curiosity and wonder bears witness to our need to ask about how we relate to life, and what its value is.

The Christian teaching of creation affirms that life is ultimately *gift*. God does not cling to being, but opens a space for otherness, for matter and life to thrive in their diversity. We do not live for ourselves alone, and we are not driven only by cold, unthinking forces. We are born into relationship. We are promised to the other, answerable to the other, before we ever say a word or make a choice. Realising that is the basis for true freedom.

God is encountered in the heart of the creative process of life. God is gift, possibility, depth, promise. God is the 'touch of transcendence'—intimately close to us, and yet never reduced to being a part of the world we can master. That touch opens us to see the image of God in every other person, and, indeed, in nonhuman creatures and creation as a whole.

Passion

I hope it is clear that the Christian God does not just snap his fingers to get the world going and then just watch it from afar. The Bible uses personal imagery to underline how much creation is a work of care, delight and liberation. God has a passion for the world.

Passion is an interesting word. We most often associate it with intense feeling, deep commitment and erotic pleasure. But in its roots it also refers to suffering (a sense that is preserved in 'compassion', meaning to feel and suffer alongside others).

This reminds us that, for Christians, God is most decisively revealed in the passion of Jesus. It is, first, a passion for life which has little time for the systems which exclude, humiliate and condemn people. As we will discover later in this book, Jesus' message and his actions made a different order of things visible. But, secondly, Jesus' passion was also his willingness to take the place of the victim, to suffer and die so that the cycle of violence and hate could be broken.

God's passion for the world is to save life, not to kill, and to draw all people to their fulfilment. It is a subversive passion, because it undermines our systems of power and control, of empire and consumerism, of personal paralysis, fear and guilt. It gives us what the Bible calls hearts of flesh, able to feel and be vulnerable once again. We are invited to follow Jesus, dying to an old way of life which is hard and brittle, and rising to embrace a new creation.

God is met in the humanity, in the flesh of Jesus. That is a scandal to our desire to keep God separate and apart from the world, in a fantasy heaven of purity and holiness. But God's is a very different kind of holiness: earthy, bodily, full of desire.

Desire

We are beginning to sense the dimensions of this vision of God. It is generous, inclusive, dynamic, personal and something that touches on our deepest experiences of meaning and purpose. It is also challenging to our fixed ideas about who is in and who is out, and about what really matters. Faith in this God should make a difference to our personal priorities, but also to the way we value people and look after creation.

It is a faith that is rooted in desire: first and foremost, God's desire for us to have and enjoy life to the full. Starting with that, we can allow our own desires to be freed from the endless pursuit of wealth, status and separation from all that threatens us. Instead, desire can become the living heart of a faith which welcomes God in the stranger.

To believe in the Holy Spirit is to allow God's desire and ours to meet. In the Bible, the Spirit empowers the weak and gives confidence to the persecuted. But the Spirit also drives people beyond their comfort zone, and guides them into new and unsuspected truths. These might be truths about ourselves that we'd rather not hear, uncomfortable truths about our cowardice, selfishness and indifference, for example.

This is not just a guilt trip, however. The Spirit moves us on, freeing us from our clinging to the past. As Jesus puts it, the Spirit is like breath or the wind: no one sees where it comes from or where it goes. The Spirit cannot be confined. It is risky to follow her call. But in doing so, we find ourselves coming to life again, as if for the first time.

No narrow dogma can determine where the Spirit will be at work. After all, the early church had to confront the fact that non-Jews were tasting the Spirit, filled with the life that broke down barriers of race, gender and status. It was confirmation that the church could only live if it were constantly being opened to the gifts brought by the other, the stranger, the foreigner.

Paul has a wonderful image of the Spirit, praying within us with sighs too deep for words. We can be caught into the unending life of relationships that God opens out to us. The church is called to be inclusive from the very start, because that is the nature of the God who invites all things into being.

The name of God

Back in the 1960s, theologians like Paul Tillich and John Robinson called upon us to take a long hard look at our images of God. They thought that talk of God being 'above us' made the divine reality too separate, to easy to turn into an irrelevance or hardened into distant cosmic dictator.

Their works struck a resonant chord at the time, but many in the churches accused them of abandoning God altogether. As a result, much theology in the Western world became more defensive, more inward-looking, more 'churchy'.

This is a great shame. As I have tried to show, Christian doctrine itself is living, open and dynamic, because it responds to a God who cannot be enclosed by our definitions. The event of God shatters our defensive barriers. No longer should we put any kind of 'sacred' violence and force on a pedestal. Instead, we are invited to share the weakness, the foolishness of God revealed as vulnerable love—and to have faith that this love is in fact stronger than anything else.

Love never dies. It is not limited. It changes everything and endures to the end. To say that 'God is love' is to let ourselves be called and shaped by this reality. It is a faith that engages us with the world more deeply. It is a passion that stands with those pushed to the margins and sacrificed by faceless powers. It is a desire that is restless, joyful, pulsing through the veins of earth and time.

Renewing this faith for today will not cause us to withdraw into the ghettoes of a religious world that only talks to itself. Instead, it will be a joyful, confident, hopeful faith, which no longer rests in the dead grip of idols. God is the name of the unnameable truth, an encounter that has to be experienced for itself. The name of God shelters a radical hope, that in all the messiness and glory of life, we will meet the One who has known us and accepted us from before the foundation of the world.

Steven Shakespeare

For reflection and discussion

What kind of idols do we fashion and how do they hinder our vision of God?
What life changing experiences shape an understanding of God?
In the wake of scientific discoveries does God inevitably become the God of the gaps?
How can Christian doctrines of Creation or Trinity help in our understanding of God?
How does belief in God make a difference?

For further reading

Marcus J.Borg, The God We Never Knew, Harper San Francisco, ISBN 0060610352

John Robinson, Honest To God, SCM Classics, with preface by David L. Edwards, ISBN 0334028515

Steven Shakespeare and Hugh Rayment-Pickard, The Inclusive God, Canterbury Press, ISBN 1853117412

God Made Simple: An SCM Basic Guide by Alison Webster (Editor), SCM Publications ISBN 0906359279

Peter Rollins, How (Not) to Speak of God, SPCK Publishing, ISBN 0281057982

Keith Ward, Pascal's Fire - Scientific Faith and Religious Understanding, One World ISBN 181684468

Karen Armstrong, A History of God, Vintage ISBN 0099273675

Howard Jones, The Thoughtful Guide to God, O Books, ISBN 1905047703

John Shelby Spong, Why Christianity Must Change or Die, Harper Collins, ISBN 0060675365

Gerard Hughes, God of Surprises, Darton, Longman and Todd, ISBN 0232527253

The Hope Seen in Jesus

Marcus J. Borg is Hundere Distinguished Professor of Religion and Culture at Oregon State University

Jesus and God

At the heart of Christianity is an affirmation about Jesus and God: Jesus is for Christians the decisive revelation of God. He is the decisive disclosure or epiphany of God.

This is the central meaning of familiar phrases from the New Testament: Jesus is the Word of God become flesh, the Wisdom of God incarnate, the Son who reveals the Father. As revealer, he is the light of the world who shines in the darkness. The conviction that Jesus is the decisive revelation of God is the foundation of orthodox Christianity to this day.

As decisive revelation of God, Jesus is the normative revelation. Though Christians also speak of the Bible as the Word of God, Jesus ultimately stands above the Bible. When the Bible and Jesus conflict, as they sometimes do, Jesus is normative. The Word of God in a person trumps the Word of God in a book.

Christianity is the only major religion to find the decisive revelation of God in a person. It is one of its distinguishing features. Its two closest relatives, Judaism and Islam, both find the decisive revelation of God in a book. Lest I be misunderstood, I emphasize that this difference is not about superiority, but about distinctiveness.

To say that Jesus is the decisive revelation of God is not to say that we see all of God in Jesus. There are aspects of God that cannot be embodied and seen in a human life. To use an obvious example, the omnipresence of God cannot be seen in a human life. To cite other traditional attributes of God, the omniscience and omnipotence of God cannot be embodied in a human life. A person who was omniscient and omnipotent would not be human, would not be one of us.

What can be seen of God in a human life is the character and passion of God. By character, I mean what we mean when we speak of the character of a human being—what that person is like at a very deep level. What is God's character? What is God like? By passion, I mean what God is passionate about, as when we ask of a person, "What is your passion"?

In Jesus, we see what a human life filled with God looks like. So we turn to the question: as the decisive revelation of what can be seen of God in a human life, what does Jesus reveal and disclose about the character and passion of God? And what does he reveal and disclose about the way to God?

Jesus

Because of Jesus' status for Christians as the decisive revelation of God, what we can glimpse of Jesus matters. Christians for many centuries knew only the Jesus of the gospels. It was enough. Read thoughtfully, carefully and prayerfully, the gospel portraits of Jesus conveyed an understanding of Jesus that nourished the lives of millions.

In our time, we have an additional resource for glimpsing Jesus, namely, the historical study of Jesus and Christian origins that began over two hundred years ago. I will describe what I think the historical study of Jesus discloses.

I begin with the importance of distinguishing between the pre-Easter Jesus and the post-Easter Jesus, between the historical Jesus and the risen living Christ. When I was young, growing up in the church, I didn't know about this distinction and perhaps wouldn't have understood it, even if I had heard about it.

As a result, I saw Jesus as more divine than human. That is because I lumped everything together that I heard about Jesus from the gospels, the creeds, Christian preaching and hymns, and so forth. Hence I thought of him, even as a historical figure, as already having the mind of God and the power of God. Because I thought of him as more divine than human, I really lost track of the utterly remarkable human being that he was.

South African Jesus scholar Albert Nolan makes the same point when he says in a quotation that I've grown fond of, "Jesus is a much underrated man. When we deprive Him of His humanity, we deprive Him of His greatness."

So what was Jesus like? I begin with my most compact summary of the pre-Easter Jesus, a three-fold summary. For those of you who know one or more of my books about Jesus, this will be familiar but I trust not too tedious.

I speak of Jesus first of all as a Jewish mystic. Mystics are people who have vivid and typically frequent experiences of God, the sacred. For a mystic, God is an experienced reality, not primarily an article of belief. Thus I see Jesus as one who knew God, who knew the Sacred, who knew the Spirit—terms which I use synonymously and interchangeably. For him, the Spirit of God was an experiential reality.

Secondly, I see the pre-Easter Jesus as a wisdom teacher. As a wisdom teacher, he taught a way, a path. I name that way, that path, with four short sentences, all of which I understand to be saying the same thing. It was a way that led beyond convention. It was the road less travelled—to use a phrase that we know from M. Scott Peck's best-selling book, who in turn borrowed it from Robert Frost. It was, to use language from Jesus himself, the narrow way, the narrow gate, in contrast is to the broad way of conventional wisdom. Fourth, and finally, it was a subversive and alternative wisdom.

The third statement: the pre-Easter Jesus was a prophet of the Kingdom of God. The Kingdom of God is for this world, as the Lord's prayer makes clear: "Your kingdom come on earth as it is already in heaven." The Kingdom of God is God's dream, God's passion, for this world.

As a prophet of God's kingdom, Jesus was like the great God-intoxicated prophets of the Jewish Bible, the Christian Old Testament. They also had vivid experiences of God and in the name of God became voices of religious and social protest directed against the domination systems of their day. Domination systems were marked by an economics of exploitation, a politics of oppression, a religion of legitimation, and the threat and use of violence. This is the world of the foreign empires that often ruled the Jewish people, as well as the world of the monarchy within Israel.

Jesus was like these prophets—a radical critic of the domination system in the Jewish homeland in His day. Indeed, it was his passion for the Kingdom of God, for a world of justice and peace, that accounts for his execution by the powers that ruled his world. He had become a radical critic of the way things were in the name of God's passion for the world. This is the political meaning of Good Friday.

To put this three-fold summary into three phases, there was to Jesus a spirit dimension, a wisdom dimension, and a justice dimension.

The Christian Life

Now, what would it mean to take Jesus seriously as the decisive disclosure or revelation of what a life full of God is like? What do we see? What would such a life look like? I will speak about this with the same three subheadings I have just named.

A Life Centered in God. First, it would be a life lived in relationship to the God whom Jesus knew in his own experience. The Christian life would not be very much about believing, and would not be about believing now for the sake of heaven later, but would be about a deepening and transforming relationship with God in the present.

This is the central meaning of spirituality. Spirituality is about becoming conscious of and intentional about our relationship to God. I say "conscious of" because I believe that we are all already in a relationship with God and have been so since our very beginning, whether we know that or not, believe that or not. Spirituality is about becoming conscious of that relationship. I say "intentional" because spirituality involves paying attention to that relationship, being intentional about deepening that relationship and letting that relationship grow. Just as human relationships grow and deepen through spending time in them and paying attention to them, so also our relationship with God grows in this same way.

Living by an Alternative Wisdom. Secondly, a life that takes Jesus seriously as a disclosure of what a life full of God is like would be a life lived by the alternative wisdom of Jesus. The alternative wisdom of Jesus, the way less travelled, is, in fact, the same as a life lived in relationship to the spirit. The wisdom of Jesus leads us into a radical centring in God, the sacred. The contrast is to the life of conventional wisdom, which is the life that most of us live most of the time.

I have described conventional wisdom a number of times in my books, so here I will be concise. Conventional wisdom is a culture's most taken-for-granted notions about two things—about what is real and about how to live. Conventional wisdom is cultural consensus; it is "what everybody knows." It is what we are socialized into as we grow up. Growing up is basically learning the categories, labels and language of the culture in which we live, and its messages about what to value and what life is about.

Living in the world of conventional wisdom has a number of consequences. I highlight two. The first: conventional wisdom blinds us to wonder. To illustrate in a simple way: imagine that you had never before in your life seen a four-legged furry creature and then you see a cat. You would be utterly fascinated. Your attention would be riveted on that cat. But because cats are familiar to us and because we have the word "cat", most often when we see a cat a little label goes on in our head that says "cat", and we don't pay any more attention to it unless it is an especially striking cat or we've got a lot of time on our hands or it is our cat. The point: conventional wisdom blinds us to the sheer wonder of what is. It makes things look ordinary and familiar and nothing special.

When you think about it, the real wonder is that the world could ever look ordinary to us. You know how remarkable it is that we are, and that there is anything, and that we are here, and that this is all around us.

There is a religious form of conventional wisdom as well. The religious form of conventional wisdom blinds us to the mystery and wonder of life with its excessive certitude about the way things are. There is also a secular form. The secular form is the reduction of reality to the visible world of our ordinary experience, which is nothing special. Secular conventional wisdom has its excessive certitude as well.

A second effect of conventional wisdom is that it tells us how to live. The central values of our culture get embedded within our minds as we grow up. One could make a very good case that the central values of modern Western culture are what I have called the three A's—appearance, affluence and achievement. All of us, at least in the first half of our lives, are, to a large extent, driven by these values. Driven by these values, we become blind to much else as well as burdened and preoccupied as to how we measure up to those values.

The way of Jesus is an invitation out of that kind of life—an invitation into a radically different kind of life. To put it abstractly, the wisdom teaching of Jesus invites us to a radical decentring and recentring: a decentring from the world of conventional wisdom and a recentring in the spirit of God. To put it less abstractly by using one of the familiar images or metaphors from the New Testament, the way of Jesus involves dying to an old way of being and being born into a new way of being. That death and rebirth are at the very centre of the Christian life; that death and rebirth are at the very centre of the season of Lent, which is really about journeying with Jesus from Galilee to Jerusalem. Jerusalem, that place of endings and beginnings, that place of death and being born again.

The way of Jesus has as its central fruit growth in compassion. Delivered from the blinkers of conventional wisdom, we become more compassionate beings. We see the wondrous creature that each of us is. We are also delivered from the preoccupation with pursuing the values of our culture that beat like a drum in our heads.

A Life Filled with God's Passion for Justice and Peace. The third is perhaps the most unfamiliar and even unsettling to many Christians. It is the justice dimension of taking Jesus seriously. The God of the Bible, as we see that God disclosed in Moses, the prophets, and Jesus, is passionate about justice and peace. Importantly, justice in the Bible is not about criminal justice, but about the just distribution of God's earth.

Why this passion for justice? Why is the God of the Bible so passionate about justice? The answer is disarmingly simple. Because God cares about human suffering and the single greatest source of unnecessary human suffering, of unnecessary social misery, is systemic injustice. By systemic injustice I mean sources of suffering caused by cultural systems, by the structures of society. This is a difficult notion for many of us to grasp because of the ethos of individualism.

So I say a bit more about systemic injustice. Think of all the suffering caused throughout history, in the ancient world and in the contemporary world, by economic exploitation and destructive impoverishment, by the way elites in every society have made the system work in their own self-interest, by political oppression, by all the isms—racism, sexism, heterosexism, nationalism, and imperialism. These are all examples of systemic injustice. Injustice is built into cultural systems.

More subtly, think of all the suffering caused by rigidly held convention and the cultural shaming that frequently goes along with it. To flesh this out with a few examples. Many of us can remember forty or fifty years ago what it was like for a young woman to become pregnant out of wedlock and the cultural shaming that went with that. Think of how until recently single adult women who didn't marry were viewed as old maids, as spinsters. Think of all the cultural shame that gay and lesbian people have experienced. All of these are examples of what I mean by systemic injustice, suffering caused by cultural systems and often legitimated by religion and in the name of God.

Jesus as prophet of the Kingdom of God, in the tradition of the great Jewish prophets, stood against the systemic injustice of His day. Taking Jesus seriously means that our own consciousness needs to be raised regarding the way in which cultural systems cause enormous suffering for people. We need to understand that the ethical imperative that flows from Jesus is both personal and political. It is both compassion and justice.

To sum this up, taking Jesus seriously means a life increasingly centred in the spirit of God, a life lived by the alternative wisdom of Jesus and a life marked by compassion and justice.

Marcus Borg

For reflection and discussion

Borg writes of Jesus as 'the decisive revelation of God' for Christians. How does this description stand alongside the term Son of God?

How helpful to you is the distinction between the pre-Easter Jesus and the post Easter Jesus? (Theologians have often spoken of the Jesus of History and the Christ of Faith.) What does this mean?

'In Jesus we see what a human life filled with God looks like' (Borg) Could this be said about other great religious figures? What is distinctive about Jesus?

For further reading

Marcus J.Borg, Meeting Jesus Again for the First Time, Harper San Francisco, ISBN 0060609176

Marcus J. Borg, Jesus: Uncovering the Life, Teachings, and Relevance of a Religious Revolutionary, Harper One ISBN 0061434345

Marcus J Borg and N. T. Wright, The Meaning of Jesus, Harper San Francsiso ISBN 0061285544 Excellent comparison of the radical and more conservative understandings of Jesus, by Borg and the Bishop of Durham

John Shelby Spong, Jesus for the Non Religious, Harper One, ISBN 0060778415

Mark Allan Powell, The Jesus Debate, Lion Hudson, currently out of print but worth trying to get a second hand copy. One of the best summaries of historians and theologians researching the historical Jesus

Barrie Wilson, How Jesus became Christian, Weidenfeld & Nicolson, ISBN 0297852000

Geza Vermes, The Changing Faces of Jesus, Penguin Books Limited, ISBN 0140265244 (and other titles about Jesus)

David Boulton, Who on Earth was Jesus? O Books, ISBN 1846940184

E P Sanders, The Historical Figure of Jesus, Penguin Books Limited, ISBN 0140144994

John Vincent, Radical Jesus, Ashram Press ISBN 0551013443

Hope for our world
God's Kingdom on Earth

John Dominic Crossan is Professor Emeritus at De Paul University, Chicago and is widely regarded as the foremost historical Jesus scholar of our time.

*T*he devil took him to a very high mountain and showed him all the kingdoms of the world and their splendour; and he said to him, "All these I will give you, if you will fall down and worship me." Jesus said to him, "Away with you, Satan! for it is written, 'Worship the Lord your God, and serve only him'" (Matthew 4:8-10).

In Matthew's version of the Gospel, both John the Baptist and Jesus the Christ announce the same message: "In those days John the Baptist appeared in the wilderness of Judea, proclaiming, 'Repent, for the Kingdom of Heaven has come near'" (Matthew 3:1-2) and "From that time Jesus began to proclaim, 'Repent, for the Kingdom of Heaven has come near'" (4:17). But is the content, meaning, and program of the Kingdom exactly the same for both of those Jewish martyrs?

Preliminaries

First, it is unfortunate that the expression *Kingdom of Heaven* ever entered the Christian vocabulary. In the New Testament it is used over 30 times but only by Matthew while *Kingdom of God* is used twice as often, and in Mark, Luke, John, Acts, and Paul. Furthermore, Matthew himself also uses *Kingdom of God* about five times. That *Kingdom of Heaven*—in Greek, actually, *Kingdom of the Heavens*—is all too often misinterpreted as the Kingdom of the future, of the next world, of the afterlife. But, for Matthew, *Heaven* was simply a euphemism for *God*, with Dwelling used for Dweller, as one could say "Downing Street announces" to mean "the Prime Minister announces." In other words, Kingdom of Heaven means exactly the same as Kingdom of God.

The Kingdom of God, therefore, is *of* heaven but not *in* heaven, *on* earth but not *of* earth. That is very clear in these parallel phrases of the Lord's Prayer in Matthew 6:10: "May your kingdom come. May your will be done, *on earth* as it is in heaven." The Kingdom of God is about the Will of God for this earth here below. My own personal translation of God's Kingdom is the Great Divine Clean-Up of the World.

Second, the Kingdom of God is not, emphatically not, about the destruction of our earth but about its transformation. It is not about the end or last things (Greek: *eschata*) of the world but about the end or last things of inequality and injustice, evil, violence, and war. It is about redeeming divine creation from human civilization. It is about taking God's world back from the thugs.

Third, the Kingdom of God is 100% political and 100% religious all together and inextricably intertwined at the same time. *Kingdom* is a political term, *God* is a religious term, and Jesus would be executed for that *of* in a Roman world where God already sat on Caesar's throne because Caesar was God Incarnate. For Jesus, the "Kingdom of God" raised a politico-religious or religio-political question: To whom did the world belong and how, therefore, should it be run?

Finally, I will be making three major comparisons between John and Jesus but that is not to exalt one martyr over another and certainly not to exalt Christianity over Judaism. Jesus owed so much to the Baptist that easy superiority is precluded. But John promised the advent of God, for example, and all that came was Antipas' cavalry. John died and still God did not come. Jesus watched, learned, and changed his vision of God. Also, John's execution protected Jesus until if and when Herod Antipas—ruler of Galilee and Perea—felt safe enough to kill another popular but dissident prophet.

God's Kingdom as imminent or present?

John. John proclaimed the imminent arrival of God's Kingdom on this earth. Any day now but certainly very soon, God would come to purify and justify an earth grown old in impurity and injustice. Roman oppression was a punishment for Israel's sins and that sinfulness impeded the promised advent of God. What was needed, therefore, was a great sacrament of repentance, a popular repetition of ancient Israel's exodus, coming from the eastern desert, crossing the Jordan river, and entering the promised land. And in that process they would repent of their sins as they were "baptized" or immersed in the Jordan with their moral cleansing symbolized by the physical washing.

A critical mass of repentant people who had "retaken" their promised land would at least prepare or possibly even hasten the start of God's Great Clean-Up. In the meanwhile, of course, and no matter how non-violent that was in theory, John was planting ticking time-bombs of divine expectation all over the Jewish homeland. So Antipas executed him. And God still did not come.

Jesus. One of the surest things we know about Jesus is that he was baptized by John. What makes it so sure is the growing nervousness that fact evokes as you move from Mark 1:9-11, through Matthew 3:13-15 and Luke 3:21, into John 1:26-33. But all of that only emphasizes that John baptized Jesus and, therefore, that Jesus had *at least originally* accepted John's message of the imminent advent of God's transformative Kingdom on this earth.

That would explain, for example, Jesus' defense of John, the desert-hardened prophet, in contrast with Antipas, the wind-shaken reed, in Luke 7:24-27. But the very next verse in 7:28 both reiterates that accolade in its first half and then drastically downgrades it in the second part: "I tell you, among those born of women no one is greater than John; yet the least in the kingdom of God is greater than he. "

Furthermore, as Jesus said of his own healing program: "if it is by the finger of God that I cast out the demons, then the kingdom of God has come to you" (Luke 11:20). In other words, Jesus started by accepting John's theology of God's *imminence* but, precisely because of what happened to John, he changed from that to a theology of God's *presence.* Jesus' own proclamation, therefore, insisted that the Kingdom of God was not imminent but present, was already here below upon this earth and, however it was to be consummated in the future, *it was a present-already and not just an imminent-future reality.*

God's Kingdom as violent or non-violent?

The question here is not whether John or Jesus were violent or advocated violent revolt. That they did not do so is evident from their fate. When confronted with violent resistance, Rome attempted to capture and execute as many of the group as possible. That is, for example, what Mark records about Barabbas, who "was in prison with the rebels who had committed murder during the insurrection" (15:7). With non-violent resistance, they executed the leader as a warning and deterrent—so Antipas for John and Pilate for Jesus.

The question, therefore, is not about human but about divine violence. Does God's Kingdom involve divine—even if exclusively divine—violence?

John. The Baptist's reply is very clear. The imminent advent is of a punitive, avenging, and violent God, as you can see in these metaphors:

John said to the crowds that came out to be baptized by him, "You brood of vipers! Who warned you to flee from the wrath to come? Bear fruits worthy of repentance ... Even now the axe is lying at the root of the trees; every tree therefore that does not bear good fruit is cut down and thrown into the fire" (Luke 3:7-9).

That language in 3:7-9,16 comes from John himself but it is humanely softened by Luke's own editorial insertion in 3:10-14:

And the crowds asked him, "What then should we do?" In reply he said to them, "Whoever has two coats must share with anyone who has none; and whoever has food must do likewise." Even he said to them, "Collect no more than the amount prescribed for you." Soldiers also asked him, "And we, what should we do?" He said to them, "Do not extort money from anyone by threats or false accusation, and be satisfied with your wages."

In one sense, of course, John was right that the Kingdom of God was imminent but it would not come as he or anyone else expected.

Jesus. The motivation given by Jesus for human non-violence is quite simply divine non-violence—even or especially when dealing with one's violent enemies. In Matthew, Jesus commands his hearers to "love your enemies and pray for those who persecute you" and the reason given is "so that you may be children of your Father in heaven; for he makes his sun rise on the evil and on the good, and sends rain on the righteous and on the unrighteous" (5:44-45). And Luke's version says to " love your enemies ... and you will be children of the Most High; for he is kind to the ungrateful and the wicked" (6:35).

Furthermore, the conclusion in Matthew is very striking. "Be perfect, therefore, as your heavenly Father is perfect" (5:48). That sounds impossible for how could the human be as perfect as the divine? But, in Greek, that verb "to be perfect" can also be translated as "to be finished"—for example, with Jesus' dying words, "It is finished," in John 9:30. In other words, we humans are perfected, finished, fully completed in our humanity, when we are non-violent in imitation of and participation in the non-violent God.

God's Kingdom as monopoly or franchise?

I put it this way so that you will remember this third and often-ignored difference between the Kingdom-program of John and of Jesus: *John had a monopoly but Jesus had a franchise.*

John. John was "the Baptist" or "the Baptizer"—that was his nickname in both Josephus and the New Testament. There were not lots of little baptizing stations all up and down the Jordan and you simply went to the one nearest your own home. You went to John and only to John. To stop his movement, therefore, Antipas had only to execute John. It might linger on in memory, nostalgia, and sorrow for one or two generations but, since it depended on John's life, it ended with John's death. Once again, I think, Jesus watched and learned. And here is how his strategy differed from that of John.

Jesus. Jesus could hardly have made such a spectacular claim about the Kingdom's non-violent presence—especially about its presence—without immediately appending another one to it. To claim an *already-present Kingdom* means that we are waiting for God, while God is waiting for us. *It is, therefore, a Collaborative, a Participatory, an Interactive Kingdom.* The Great Divine Clean-Up of the World is a cooperation between the human and divine worlds and without both together it does not exist. Furthermore, it is a process with a present beginning in time and a future—be it short or long—consummation. Would it happen without God? No. Would it happen without believers? No. To see the presence of the Kingdom of God, said Jesus, come, see how we live, and then live likewise.

But that presumes a *communal* program, it presumes that Jesus did not just have a vision or a theory but a praxis and a program—and a program not just for himself but for others as well. What was it?

Basically, this: *heal the sick, eat with those you heal, and announce the Kingdom's presence in that mutuality.* You can see that communal program at work when Jesus sends out his companions, in such texts as Mark 6:7-13 and Luke 9:1-6 or Matthew 10:5-14 and Luke 10:1-11.

There are some very unusual features of those texts. First, Jesus himself does not settle down at Nazareth or Capernaum and send his companions to bring people to him as monopolist of the Kingdom. Second, he tells others to do exactly what he himself is doing—healing the sick, eating with the healed, and proclaiming the Kingdom's presence. Third, he does not tell them to heal in his name or even to pray to God before they heal—nor does he himself pray before he heals. That is actually quite extraordinary and can only be explained by the Kingdom's presence and their participation in it—if you are in the already-present Kingdom you are already in union with God and can act accordingly.

That logic of Jesus' Kingdom program is a mutuality of healing—as the basic spiritual power—and eating—as the basic physical power—shared freely and openly. That process built *share*-community from the bottom up as a positive alternative to Antipas' Roman *greed*-community established from the top down.

That food is the material basis of life and that the control of eating controls all else is clear enough. Even if we are normally well-fed, we realize our absolute dependence on food before all else—after that is furnished, there is much else needed but, first and foremost, no food, no life. So eating as basic physical power is relatively clear but healing as spiritual power is much more difficult to understand.

It is quite clear that Jesus was a great healer and, however we explain that capacity, its actuality seems securely certain. In his famous 1980 book, *Patients and Healers in the Context of Culture*, Arthur Kleinman emphasized that:

"A key axiom in medical anthropology is the dichotomy between two aspects of sickness: disease and illness. *Disease* refers to a malfunctioning of biological and/or psychological processes, while the term *illness* refers to the psychosocial experience and meaning of perceived disease. Illness includes secondary personal and social responses to the primary malfunctioning (disease) in the individual's physiological or psychological status (or both) ... Viewed from this perspective, illness is the shaping of disease into behavior and experience. It is created by personal, social, and cultural reactions to disease." (page 72)

And *curing* goes with disease while *healing* goes with illness. Sometimes a disease can be cured but very often the best that is possible is to heal the illness that surrounds it. That was especially true for ancient medicine but is still very often true today especially for chronic or terminal pain.

The best way to understand that distinction is to consider the movie *Philadelphia* in 1993. You will recall that Tom Hanks plays Andrew Beckett, a gay lawyer fired by his law-firm because his AIDS infection comes from homosexuality. We all understood that Beckett's *disease* (AIDS) cannot be *cured* but, as the story unfolds, we can also see that his *illness* is being *healed* by the support of his partner, his family, and his lawyer's successful suit against his law-firm's illegal discrimination. *Curing* is not available but *healing* is still possible. It is not everything, to be sure, but neither is it nothing.

The healing of illness by Jesus and his companions must be understood in the framework of the Kingdom of God's Great Cosmic Clean-Up of the World. Do not be surprised, of course, if a great and famous healer, like Jesus or Asklepios, is reputed to raise the dead, that is, to bring life emphatically and triumphantly out of death. Do not be surprised if you find it in the advertisements of their followers but be very surprised if you find it in the testimonials of their patients.

Here, in summary conclusion, is all of this in episcopal aphorisms from either end of Africa and across a millennium and a half. Augustine, Bishop of Hippo: "God made you without you … he doesn't justify you without you." Desmond Tutu, Archbishop Emeritus of Cape Town: "St Augustine says, 'God, without us, will not; as we, without God, cannot.' Incredible God. Without us, God will not."

John Dominic Crossan
Professor Emeritus of Religious Studies
DePaul University, Chicago, IL, USA

For reflection and discussion

Do you agree with Crossan's view that for Jesus the kingdom of God was not imminent but present, not about the destruction of the world but its transformation?

What would the 'Great Divine Clean-Up of the World' mean for you?

Can the use of violence ever be justified in doing the will of God?

'The Kingdom of God …is a communal program at work' (Crossan) What for you would be the main elements of that program?

For further reading

John Dominic Crossan, God and Empire: Jesus Against Rome, Then and Now, Harper San Francisco, ISBN 0060843233

Richard A. Horsley, Jesus and Empire: The Kingdom of God and the New World Disorder, Augsburg Fortress, ISBN 080063490X

John Dominic Crossan and Jonathan L. Reed, In Search of Paul, Harper One, ISBN 0060816163

Joachim Jeremias, The Parables of Jesus, SCM Press, ISBN 0334029171

Walter Wink, The Powers That Be (and other Wink titles), Bantam Doubleday Dell, ISBN 0385487525

Marcus J.Borg, The Heart of Christianity, Harper Collins ISBN 0060730684

Jim Wallis, Seven Ways to Change the World, (and other Wallis titles) Lion Hudson

Hope through the Scriptures

Keith Ward is Professor of Divinity, Gresham College, London and Regius Professor of Divinity Emeritus, University of Oxford

I n the beginning was the Word' (John 1:1). For Christians, the Word of God is not a written text, the Bible, but the living person of Jesus Christ. That is the definitive key to a truly Christian interpretation of the Bible. Without the Bible, we would not know what Jesus was remembered to have done and said. We would not know the Jewish context of prophetic expectation in which he lived. We would not see how human perceptions of God developed from the tribal war-god of the early Hebrew tribes to the God of unlimited love who was seen in Jesus. The Bible is an essential text for Christians, and there is something to learn from every part of it.

'All Scripture is God-breathed and is useful for teaching, rebuking, correcting and training in righteousness' (2 Timothy 3:16). But two points must be noted. First, the word 'God-breathed' (*theopneustos*) is not the same as 'God-dictated'. In the Book of Genesis, the spirit (the 'breath') of God swept over the waters of the formless void (Gen 1:2). And God breathed into the nostrils of the first humans 'the breath of life' (Gen 2:7). The universe at its origin, humans and indeed all animals, are God-breathed. God arouses life and order out of chaos and lifelessness. So when Scripture is God-breathed, it becomes, by the action of the Spirit, a source of life and wisdom. That does not mean that God actually dictated it, so that there are no human errors or no different points of view or no developments of understanding in the text.

The second point is that the Bible does indeed contain many different views. The Book of Job depicts the great suffering of an innocent man, while Psalm 37 says, 'I have been young, and now am old, yet I have not seen the righteous forsaken or their children begging bread' (verse 25). These are very different views of the suffering of the innocent. We can only account for this difference by saying that they represent very partial human responses to life before God.

In a similar way, Psalm 6 says, 'In death there is no remembrance of you' (verse 5), while Jesus said that God 'is God not of the dead, but of the living; for to him all of them are alive' (Luke 20:38). There is a clear development within the Bible from an early belief in *Sheol*, as a gloomy place of the dead, to the New Testament proclamation of resurrection to eternal life.

The idea of God, too, develops from early parts of the Bible, written in the Bronze Age, where God is one tribal God of war among others, to the teaching of second Isaiah that there is only one creator of all things, a God of justice and mercy. This idea of God is developed further again by Jesus, who teaches that the Creator is a God of unlimited love and forgiveness.

So if the Bible is read carefully, it can be seen to contain many different and partial viewpoints, and to record a development in the ideas of God and salvation that is, for Christians, completed and transformed by Jesus. It is only when the text is taken as a whole, and when Jesus is taken as the central key for interpreting it, that it becomes useful for teaching. We should not take any text in isolation. And as Christians we must interpret every text in the light of the Gospel records of Jesus.

Seen in the light of Jesus, much that we learn from the Bible is about human failures to understand God, and limitations of vision that were only slowly— and perhaps never entirely—overcome. If the person of Jesus—healing, forgiving, reconciling, condemning religious arrogance, consorting with the poor, and calling all to the way of love—is our key to interpreting the Bible, then much of the Bible stands condemned. Slaughtering Amalekites, putting-away of non-Jewish wives, stoning disobedient sons to death, and praying for the murder of the children of one's enemies—all these things are to be found in the Bible, but are roundly condemned by the Sermon on the Mount.

Faith in Christ compels us to read the Bible, therefore, as a developing record of imperfect human responses to God. All Scripture is useful for teaching. But what it often teaches is how prejudiced and short-sighted people are—a useful reminder to us that we too are prejudiced and myopic. Reading the Bible teaches us that God leads us slowly towards truth, but we resist to a quite remarkable extent.

The Bible, for Christians, is not the dictated words of God; it is the witness to the personal Word of God. Each part of it must be read in a way that points to the fulness of Christ. That is the first principle of a Christian interpretation of the Bible. The second principle follows from it. If the Bible is to be read as pointing to Christ, that means often taking it in a symbolic or spiritual, rather than a literal, sense. We can, for instance, take the command to exterminate Amalekites to point to the need for complete devotion to God and total opposition to sin. But we cannot forget that the literal sense is morally abhorrent, a command of genocide. To interpret such passages we need to be free to reject their literal sense, but also to see them as stages in developing ideas about God which are continually revised throughout the Bible and which, however perversely, point forward to a deeper understanding of God, decisively revealed in Christ, though still not fully understood by us.

So a sense of history is needed, as we read the Bible. A strong sense of metaphor, of the way in which literal images can stand for spiritual teachings, is equally important. God does not literally ride on the clouds, and God is not literally 'up' in the sky. Such physical images represent God's majesty and sovereignty. The earth is not, as Genesis supposes, a flat disc floating on a cosmic sea, with the sun, moon and stars hung from the bowl of the sky. We need a sense of poetry, to find deep spiritual meaning in these mythical and literally false symbols. The sea, for example, represents the threatening and chaotic elements of the universe, and the garden of Eden ('bliss') represents the beauty of the natural world, for which humans are responsible. It is tragic that literalist interpreters of the Bible seem to have lost this sense of symbolism, and turn the imagery of the Book of Revelation into a timetable of physical events in the near future. Throughout the Bible, historical events are used as images of eternal or spiritual truths. Of course, we can take quite a lot of historical narratives in the Bible literally—though even there, the literal details are not of primary importance. But the vital questions to ask are: what is the spiritual truth these things express? Why did the editors of the Gospels, for example, choose just these events, describe them in just this way, and put them in just this order?

To help in answering these questions, the Gospels should always be read with the aid of a synopsis and a good commentary. Lay them alongside one another, noting the differences and similarities, and ask: what does this show us about the way the editor saw the life of Jesus? About what he thought was important, and what response Jesus was evoking in him? Comparing Mark and John, we cannot fail to see huge differences of response to one who is the same person, Jesus. In Mark, Jesus speaks in short cryptic sentences, and tells the disciples not to tell anyone that he is the Messiah. In John, Jesus speaks in long discourses, and openly declares that he is the Son of God, the light of the world. What accounts for these differences? We will quickly discover that scholars differ in their suggestions, but they all agree that the questions are inescapable. Maybe the reason for that is that we should see that there are, and always have been, different ways of seeing Jesus. They have been there from the very first, illustrated by the fact that we have four Gospels, and it is positively misleading to try to collapse the different Gospels into one literal biography. That would miss the point, which is that the Gospels record very personal responses to God as revealed in Jesus. When we see this, we can have the freedom to make our own, perhaps different, personal response. And that is what the Bible should be, a diverse, developing sets of texts that embody a personal divine address inviting us to make our own unique response, not a set of facts that we just have to accept without question.

The besetting sin of Biblical interpretation is the failure to accept that there exist many diverse interpretations of the texts. There is no 'one true' understanding, though of course some interpretations are more adequate than others. We must take our own view, but it should be an instructed view. A view of the Bible is instructed if it takes into account the range of reputable Biblical scholarship that is represented in, for example, the Oxford Bible commentary. Not everyone needs to read the Oxford Bible Commentary, though probably if you can, it is a Christian duty to do so. Yet every Christian should have a great deal of regard for the views of those who have spent their lives studying the texts in the original languages, and who know all that patient scholarship which has accumulated in the last 200 years. I am not suggesting that the Oxford Bible Commentary has it right. I am suggesting that it gives a necessary background to forming personal views about how God reveals the divine nature and purpose in Jesus.

So in reading the Bible, we need a sense of history, of the historical contexts in which the documents were written, and of the developing history of the basic Biblical ideas of God, salvation, and revelation. We need a sense of poetry, of how literal-sounding statements can convey implicit and many-sided spiritual insights into the relation of finite beings to the infinite mystery of

God. We need some knowledge of modern Biblical scholarship in all its diversity, or at the very least an acceptance that such scholarship is an aid to discerning divine truth, and not an invention of the Devil. And we need above all a personal devotion to Jesus Christ, the one to whom the Bible witnesses, in many developing, imperfect, yet potentially illuminating, ways.

The Bible is a pillar of Christian faith, but it should be read in the knowledge that 'we serve in the new way of the Spirit, and not in the old way of the written code' (Romans 7:6). The Bible is a written code, and without it we would have no access to the new life of the Spirit in Jesus, for we would not know what Jesus did and said. But it is the new way of the Spirit in which we live, and all written codes, including the Bible, must be judged, and sometimes found wanting, by the test of whether they point to the liberation of new life in the Spirit, or rather to the bondage of some written code, even if it is in the Bible itself, from which Christ has set us free.

Keith Ward

For reflection and discussion

'All Scripture is God-breathed' (2 Timothy 3.16). How do you understand this phrase in a way which makes sense for you?

Ward says that, 'Faith in Christ compels us to read the Bible ...as a developing record of imperfect human responses to God'. Do you agree and are there parts of scripture which offer glimpses of what perfect human responses to God might be?

How would you respond to the question, 'Are you a Bible believing Christian?'

For further reading

Keith Ward, What the Bible Really Teaches: A Challenge to Fundamentalists, SPCK Publishing, ISBN 0281056803

Marcus Borg, Reading the Bible Again for the First Time, HarperSanFrancisco, ISBN 0060609192

Richard Holloway, How to read the Bible, Granta Books, ISBN 1862078939

John Shelby Spong, The Sins of Scripture, HarperOne, ISBN 0060778407

Karen Armstrong, The Bible: The Biography, Atlantic Books, ISBN 1843543974

The Oxford Bible Commentary by John Barton and John Muddiman, Editors, Oxford University Press, ISBN 0199277184

Hope for Church
in the 21st Century

Jill Sandham is the honorary secretary of the Progressive Christianity Network – Britain, and Diocesan Safeguarding Adviser for the Diocese of Southwark. She is a member of St Faith's Church, North Dulwich, London.

Hugh Dawes is the chair of the Progressive Christianity Network – Britain, and an ordained priest in the Church of England. He is also a member of St Faith's Church, North Dulwich, London.

It's Maundy Thursday evening in our South London church, and we meet to share in a Seder meal and to break bread as Jesus did on his last evening with his friends. Schools have broken up for their short Easter break just a few hours before. But still more than forty of us are sitting there around one large table set in the centre of the nave.

Looking now for hope for church in the twenty-first century (we use the word 'church' very deliberately *without* the usual definite article), this feels as good a starting point as any. The meal and its symbols speak powerfully as the evening moves on, and we light candles, read stories, raise cups of wine, wash the hands of others, and eat food. They speak of our human history—of our being rooted in Judaism, but beyond that rooted also in the universal human experience from earliest times of the significance of food shared together. They speak of our Christian origins, of that new life which we share and call resurrection—rooted in the birth, life and death of Jesus. They speak too of ourselves as church rooted here and now in this place—our common life built on companionship and eucharist and worked out in care and concern. Together they tell us what church can be, if we want it to.

No-one round this table is greater than any other; no one is the greatest. Authority here is very deliberately dispersed and shared by all, so that each finds freedom to contribute on equal terms. We serve one another, and have the grace to be served. We talk, we listen, we attend and give attention. We look to our neighbours around and across the table, and we see snapshots of one another—the 'Josh-ness' of Josh, the 'Mike-ness' of Mike, the 'Freda-ness' of Freda—and somehow in this process we each discover more about who we are—the 'me-ness' of me.

We act out together in this gathered expression of our life a celebration of the ordinary: through relationships; in a meal shared; by talking and singing together. And we do so with a deep understanding of sacrament, as we pass to one another the bread and the wine. The understanding can be grasped—and caught—from the youngest (aged 3) to the oldest (aged 87) and across cultures, ethnicities and abilities. It is worth it, and we have worth, and somehow we bless each other and are blessed.

What does this teach us? Certainly that if church is to be a cause of hope and a place in which hope can be encountered and experienced, it needs to be both local and small enough to be intimate, but also sufficiently large and brave to embrace human difference and diversity as well. Holding the two together provides a human and humane alternative both to the impersonality of such a lot of public life in twenty-first century western culture, and to the non-threatening, isolating narrowness of so much that passes as private life. Not so much a counter-culture, it offers a different lens—indeed a prism—through which to view the world and our human life within it.

This has to be worked at. Churches can easily become exclusive clubs for the like-minded—we know plenty that are. But at its best the local Christian community serves as a place in which very different people feel that they belong, as much for others as for themselves: a place where conflict and disagreement are held and struggled with; and where only abuse and the misuse and imbalance of power are not welcomed or tolerated.

Church has, we have said, both its story and a history, and these things properly matter. But church must not be tied by every detail of its history, or feel trapped and weighed down by the burdens of the past. We take seriously the words L P Hartley placed at the front of his novel *The Go-Between*—"The past is another country. They do things differently there." Church lives in the present, a present different to that of our forebears. It is to the present that we must attend. The playwright Denis Potter, in an interview with Melvyn Bragg shortly before his death in 1994, spoke about the celebration of 'nowness', which expresses something of this:

"Things are both more trivial than they ever were, and more important than they ever were, and the difference between the trivial and the important doesn't seem to matter. But the nowness of everything is absolutely wondrous, and if people could see that, you know. There's no way of telling you; you have to experience it, but the glory of it, if you like, the comfort of it, the reassurance ... not that I'm interested in reassuring people—bugger that. The fact is, if you see the present tense, boy do you see it! And boy can you celebrate it."

In that wondrous nowness of our present, at one and the same time trivial and yet utterly important, church pitches its tent. We set a stage there, and create a space in our ordinary lives in which to know such moments. But these are always gifts rather than possessions, and cannot be locked or held beyond their duration. As a hymn of Sydney Carter so aptly comments:

"Catch the bird of heaven,

lock him in a cage of gold;

look again tomorrow,

and he will be gone."

Local church, renewed in the twenty-first century, has real purpose. First, church exists as a community to give fresh life to the Christian story, and so be a people, a place, where all seek, learn, experience and glimpse God's Kingdom on earth. Second, church has a duty to be prophetic in its understanding of the world, and so in its understanding of itself as well. How it organises itself, and how those who make it up treat one another, these need to ring true. Our common life has to demonstrate the conviction that all have a contribution to make, and all have a right to receive on equal terms, since each member carries the stamp and the mark of Jesus. And third, church needs, in common with other communities of faith, to be about the business of making holy the ordinary, and of ending the false divide between 'sacred' and 'secular'. Because everything is 'holy' just as it is also 'ordinary', if we only know where and how to look.

This vision for the local expression of church and what it can be is much closer actually to the model of first century church than that of Christianity's later history. But for most people of course, that model is not what the word 'church' most immediately brings to mind. 'Church' with its regular definite article means 'the institutional church'. And sadly few would recognise what we propose from what that institution has mostly become. Rather than being open to the ever-changing now, Christianity for hundreds of years has had a fixation with self-preservation and justification—and the power of those controlling it. In pursuit of that it has damned and damaged people of other faith understandings and of its own; tearing itself apart regularly, and waging internal warfare on those who read the story differently.

In reaction to that history, it is hardly surprising that in the twentieth century institutional Christianity became so preoccupied with the pursuit and recovery of unity. We who write shared in that ourselves, and were excited by it. But the liberation all too quickly turned sour. In the hands of institutional Christianity, unity, which briefly seemed so exciting and so possible, got twisted into a concern for uniformity of a narrowly doctrinal and credal form. With the result that today the institutional church can appear more divided and distorted than ever before.

We believe hope in the twenty-first century means calling time upon the old ways of institutional church, and fashioning instead a gentler 'associational' church. The old hierarchical model had popes, bishops, moderators or equivalent at the top of the triangle, with their authority cascading downwards to the local (parish) churches which sat on the triangle's long base edge. And certainly this is how the world works. Western society's model of authority, even in democracies, uses power to enforce obedience. We may manage that without the brutality of Jesus' time, but this remains power imposed from above. The chief executive and the board govern the workers. Institutional church governs largely through the clergy in much the same way.

But this is neither the style nor the way of Jesus. To recapture his insights, church has to set hierarchy and headship aside, and redefine what is meant by authority. The model of authority enacted by Jesus throughout his life and in the events leading to his death is not that of something imposed by the strong, but is rather something freely granted and bestowed by others. Without power to command, it works by influence and inspiration. We follow and learn from those whose opinions, knowledge and judgements we trust and respect. This Christian style of community depends upon trust; even at times, indeed especially at times, of disagreement and dissention. Those with authority in twenty-first century church will be those who have earned it in this way, so that authority will move regularly and freely between and among those in its communities.

Local church provides the pattern for what associational church can be. For at its best it is not fixated with the desire to hold everything together; it is untidy, disparate, holds tensions and difference, and yet finds in all of that a togetherness which is generous rather than restricting, limiting or excluding. Local church with its powerlessness finds in that its strength. An associational church—freed from institutionalism—should overcome anxiety about appearing powerless and vulnerable; and recognise that in trying to follow in the way of Jesus these are actually its strengths.

We know this will frighten some, and appears new and threatening to our comfort zones. But it does not have to be frightening. Nor need it be—and it must not become—an anarchic model. Anarchy does not keep people safe, does not create communities of participation and contribution. There will still be a need for order, through guidelines and requirements. One of us is currently struggling to write safeguarding procedures for her diocese which offer churches the tools to be and do their very best for both those who are vulnerable, and those who pose risk, living in the same community. It is very hard to frame guidelines in ways which don't read as imposing—but such guidelines only come alive as local churches struggle with these tensions and issues in their daily, ordinary living.

So what do we have to lose to come closer to that church for which we hope? First, the folly of thinking that we hold the one and only truth. More modestly we are communities who grasp truths, in common with people in other faith communities and those who are not part of any faith community. We must lose the arrogance of thinking we have the monopoly of God's love. The love is in all—the work of the people of church is to enable others to discover it freely and on their own terms, with no requirement to become 'like us'. We can work as church in association with many others, welcome the difference that involves us in, and not feel threatened by it.

Next we need to lose many of our words. The very word 'God', for a start, is a stumbling block to many both within and beyond church, with its resonating historic symbolisms of headship, wrath, masculinity and personhood. Marcus Borg, in his book *The Heart of Christianity* points helpfully to words of Thomas Keating, a key figure in the Centering Prayer Movement, speaking in a lecture

Continued on page 57

 # Changing Attitude

WORKING FOR GAY, LESBIAN, BISEXUAL & TRANSGENDER AFFIRMATION WITHIN THE ANGLICAN COMMUNION

Our Goal: The day when the Anglican Churches fully accept, welcome and offer equality of opportunity to lesbian, gay, bisexual and transgender people.

Changing Attitude England, founded in 1995, is a network of lesbian, gay, bisexual, transgender and heterosexual members of the Church of England. We welcome as members everyone whose concern is to work for change in the church's understanding of human sexuality.

We aim to move forward the debate about human sexuality in the Anglican Church by: Raising awareness; Providing education; Introducing our experience; Building relationships

We have a growing network of active diocesan groups meeting and holding events in 23 English dioceses, with contacts in 15 others, and Changing Attitude networks in Australia, Ireland, New Zealand, Nigeria and Scotland.

For further information contact:
Revd Colin Coward, 6 Norney Bridge, Mill Road, Marston, Devizes, Wiltshire, SN10 5SF, tel 01380 724908

website: www.changingattitude.org.uk
email: colin@changingattitude.org

christian aid

Christian Aid is the official development agency of more than 40 denominations in Britain and Ireland. For more than 60 years we have worked with churches to make a difference to millions of lives around the world.

We are challenged by the stark reality of an unjust world and guided by the inspiration of the Christian faith we recognise the gospel message of hope for this world - we believe in life before death.

Our work is guided by three aims:

To deliver real, practical benefits on the ground

Regardless of ethnicity, nationality or religion we work where the need is greatest. We work alongside around 700 local organisations - who know best how to deliver what people really need to ease suffering and stop poverty.

Our partners undertake a variety of programmes - from helping farmers in Kyrgyzstan increase the productivity of their land, to building storm shelters in cyclone prone Bangladesh.

To speak out where there is injustice

We aim to break the cycle of poverty by challenging the systems and structures that keep people poor. From global trade rules, to inequality in community governance - we work to encourage the powerful to consider the least powerful.

To campaign for change

Christian Aid is a movement for change - with nearly 100,000 campaigners, and hundreds of thousands of supporters - we reject a status quo that says poverty is inevitable.

This is a movement that is not afraid to tell governments, companies and institutions what they need to do to address poverty. We encourage them to change so the poverty we see is not made worse by the policies of the rich world.

If you would like to become part of this movement for change - by praying, taking action or fundraising, take a look at our website **www.christianaid.org.uk**

There you will find information about our ongoing work, our latest campaigns and resources to help you talk about global issues in churches, youth groups and schools.

C O U R A G E

The ministry of Courage UK offers a place of understanding and support for lesbian & gay people who wish to follow the path of Christian discipleship. Their families can benefit as well. Courage also offers a national resource to help churches understand the issues and needs of homosexual people.

Our aim is to seek God to find an honourable and practical way forward, consistent with Scripture, for Christian people who are also gay; to inform our brothers and sisters in our Churches who find gay issues hard to understand or accept, and to communicate the Good News to all who do not know Christ.

For further enquiries about the work of Courage please write to Jeremy Marks at:

COURAGE
P.O. Box 748
GUILDFORD, GU1 2ZY
United Kingdom
Telephone: 01484 301411

Web site: http://www.courage.org.uk

E-mail: office@courage.org.uk

C O U R A G E

THE CLERGY CONSULTATION
www.clergyconsultation.co.uk

A confidential support organisation for lesbian, gay, bisexual, transgender and intersex (lgbti) Ministers, Religious and Ordinands, and their partners, primarily from the Anglican Churches of the United Kingdom, but also welcoming member churches of CCBTI, and lgbti leaders of other faith communities and their partners.

The Clergy Consultation developed from a support network for gay priests founded in 1976 by three Church of England clergy – Malcolm Johnson, Peter Ellers and Douglas Rhymes – and a recent members' survey highlighted mutual support as the primary motive for joining.

The Clergy Consultation holds a day conference with speakers at least twice a year, often, but not always, in London. An opportunity for members to engage in theological reflection about issues of gender and sexuality, and to dialogue with invited guests, meetings always include the Eucharist, Lunch, and Tea, and sometimes entertainment.

Church leaders and theologians address the Clergy Consultation knowing that they will not be quoted afterwards as meetings are conducted by Chatham House Rules.

Sexual Ethics, Edited by Andrew Henderson, (Changing Attitude, 2004) is the report of a Clergy Consultation working party.

The Clergy Consultation is facilitated by two co-convenors (one male, one female) and a steering committee, all of whom are elected by the annual meeting, and who can be contacted on steering@clergyconsultation.org

The Clergy Consultation Mission Statement:

What is our passion?
As Ministers of the Gospel we celebrate and affirm our full humanity as sexual and spiritual beings.

What are our resources?
An inheritance of integrity and trustworthiness in which we share the experience, theology, spirituality, and pain of our members.

What are our aspirations?
To encourage and support one another as we emerge into the fullness of our humanity and sexual identities.
To incarnate the Gospel to the Church and Society at large.

The Evangelical Fellowship
for Lesbian and Gay Christians

Since its foundation in 1979 the Fellowship has provided an opportunity for lesbian, gay and bisexual Christians, mainly from an evangelical background, to meet and share experiences with other; to support and be supported in times of difficulty or stress; to encourage one another in the Christian faith; to think through issues relating both to faith and sexuality.

In addition to offering pastoral support, the Fellowship is available to facilitate discussion of sexuality in evangelical churches, and also seeks to bring the good news of God's love to the wider lesbian, gay and bisexual population.

The Fellowship runs two weekend conferences each year, to which non members are welcome. We have published some booklets and are distributor of `Reluctant Journey: A pilgrimage from homophobia to Christian love' by George Hopper, an exploration of the Biblical texts often used to condemn lesbian and gay people.

For further information contact

Pam Gold, Co Convenor, 31 Freshfields Drive, Padgate, Warrington, Cheshire, WA2 0UE, tel 01925 851187.

Website: www.eflgc.org.uk
E-mail: infor@eflgc.org.uk

FREE TO BELIEVE

In 1996 Donald Hilton and Martin Camroux organised a conference at Windermere called "Taking our liberal past into the future". This was envisaged as a one off event but out of it grew an informal network of liberal and progressive members of the URC called **FREE TO BELIEVE**. Today **FREE TO BELIEVE** has come of age:

The network now consists of over 400 people - including many from other denominations.

Each year there is a national conference (recent speakers have included Jack Spong, Keith Ward and Brian Wren) and a theological reading party.

A 20 page magazine, the 'Briefing', goes out to all members 3 times a year.

There is a growing series of booklets analysing contemporary theological issues from a progressive viewpoint (currently 11 are in print). These include:

Martin Camroux	*Coming Out as a Liberal*
Martin Camroux	*Why we must say No to Fundamentalism*
John Hick	*Is Christianity the Only True Religion, or one among others?*
Donald Hilton	*My Testimony: the Origins of a Liberal Faith*
Colin Thompson	*Homosexuality: A New Basis for Discussion*

All £2.50 from FREE TO BELIEVE

FREE TO BELIEVE is not a caucus or a faction, and is open to anyone interested in keeping Christianity a thinking and open faith.

Free to Believe is a hopeful sign of vitality and growth in the Church. While all eyes are on church decline, a new way of being liberal and Christian is emerging.

Contact us via

Revd Martin Camroux,
35 Arundel Road,
Cheam, Surrey SM2 6EU

m.camroux.t21@btinternet.com
www.freetobelieve.org.uk

Semper Reformanda!

Inclusive Church is a network of individuals and organisations whose make-up reflects the breadth and scope of the Church of England and beyond.

We come from differing traditions and differing locations but we are united in one aim: to celebrate and maintain the traditional inclusivity and diversity of the Anglican Communion. At this time more than ever we celebrate the links across continents between Anglicans. The gospel of inclusion needs to be courageously and confidently proclaimed so that we can speak truly to the needs and hopes of the world in which we live.

Inclusive Church celebrates the Anglican tradition of generous orthodoxy, and since its inception in 2003 has received considerable support from those who are concerned about the rise of increasingly harsh rhetoric that seeks to define the limits of inclusion and exclude those who disagree.

We work closely with a large number of partner organisations and hope to strengthen links with individuals and groups throughout the Communion who share our commitment to classical, generous Anglicanism.

Website: www.inclusivechurch2.net
Email: info@inclusivechurch.net

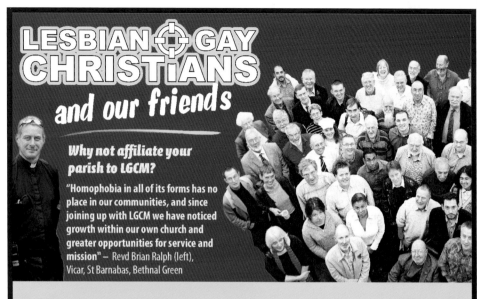

Living Spirituality Network

The Well at Willen,
Newport Road,
Milton Keynes
MK15 9AA
Email: spirituality@ctbi.org.uk
Tel: 01908 200675

The Living Spirituality Network (LSN) exists for people who are exploring the meaning of spirituality both within and beyond the traditional churches. LSN provides supporters with information, contacts and encouragement as they seek to understand and deepen their spiritual lives.

While many people pursue their spiritual quest within the traditional Christian churches, finding a rich and satisfying resource in their teaching, services and structures, the spiritual and religious landscape is changing dramatically. Some people continue to participate in church services and groups, but find most of their spiritual needs met outside them. Many spiritual seekers today have little or no experience of formal religion, and for significant numbers of others, traditional religion provides neither a context nor a language which is helpful or meaningful on their journey. Others are looking for new ways to engage with the ancient wisdom of the past, while others still are directing their spiritual energies into justice and peace or environmental initiatives, the creation of new communities, or the arts. As these different people explore and deepen their spiritual experience, practice and commitment, many of them are looking for information and for companionship. They seek access to new thinking, new ways of seeing and new experiences, and for new opportunities to connect with fellow travellers - kindred spirits - embarked on a similar quest. It is these people, primarily, whom LSN hopes to serve and support.

Living Spirituality Network - the Vision

- To be an open space for theological reflection and exploration
- To ask questions which deepen and challenge and move us forward
- To 'fly kites'
- To live the tensions that arise in spirituality
- To listen and respond to the people the churches do not meet – both inside and outside the churches

LSN works in a number of ways

- Reading the *signs of the times* and sharing newly emerging information, analysis, insights and experience in the field of spirituality and religion
- Serving as a conduit for contacts and information and providing resources: we support a well-stocked library at our base in Milton Keynes and distribute *Living Spirituality News* three times a year
- Meeting our supporters at our Gatherings, which explore important aspects of contemporary spirituality and offer the opportunity to meet like-minded people from all over Britain and Ireland
- Networking with individuals, groups and other networks with similar interests and aims

Director: Eley McAinsh
Administrator: Win Kennedy

Living the Questions

People know that at its core, Christianity has something good to offer the human race. At the same time, many have a sense that they are alone in being a "thinking" Christian and that "salvaging" Christianity is a hopeless task.

What is needed is a safe environment where people have permission to ask the questions they've always wanted to ask but have been afraid to voice for fear of being thought a heretic.

Living the Questions produces DVD-based programmes to stimulate small-group discussion, for both seekers and "church alumnae".

Titles include:
Living the Questions 2 ■ Saving Jesus ■ Eclipsing Empire ■ Jesus for the Non-Religious ■ Victory & Peace or Justice & Peace? ■ Questioning Capital Punishment ■ Paul: an Appealing or Appalling Apostle? ■ Tex Mix ■ Countering Pharaoh's Production ■ Consumption Society Today

More details and all titles are available in the UK from:
Richard Titford
2 Chestnut Mews, Friars' Street
SUDBURY, Suffolk CO10 2AH
Tel & Fax 01787 880303
Email: titford@keme.co.uk
Website: www.livingthequestions.com

The

Modern Churchpeople's Union

The MCU (Modern Churchpeople's Union) is an Anglican society which promotes liberal theology and offers Christian debate and discussion on religious issues. It embraces the spirit of free and informed enquiry and seeks to involve the Christian faith in an ongoing search for truth by interpreting traditional doctrine in the light of present day understanding. To this end it believes in open discussion, critical scholarship and willingness to change. It holds an annual conference on contemporary issues. Membership includes subscription to the journal *Modern Believing*. Its President is John Saxbee, Bishop of Lincoln.

Contact details:
General enquiries:
Jonathan Clatworthy, General Secretary
Modern Churchpeople's Union
MCU Office, 9 Westward View, Liverpool L17 7EE, UK
0845 345 1909/(+44)(0)151 726 9730
office@modchurchunion.org
www.modchurchunion.org

Membership applications:
Mr David Marshall
15 Morledge, MATLOCK
Derbyshire, DE4 3SB
01629 583958
membership@modchurchunion.org

Progressive Christianity Network – Britain

The **Progressive Christianity Network – Britain** recognises the value and significance of tradition and the scriptures in the shaping of Christian faith. It takes the following eight points not as a statement of faith, but as an expression of how we live as Christians.

We are Christians who...

Have found an approach to God through the life and teachings of Jesus;

Recognise the faithfulness of other people who have other names for the gateway to God's realm, and acknowledge that their ways are true for them, as our ways are true for us;

Understand the sharing of bread and wine in Jesus' name to be a representation of an ancient vision of God's feast for all peoples;

Invite all people to participate in our community and worship life without insisting that they become like us in order to be acceptable (including but not limited to):

> *believers and agnostics*
> *conventional Christians and questioning sceptics*
> *women and men*
> *those of all sexual orientations and gender identities*
> *those of all races and cultures*
> *those of all classes and abilities*
> *those who hope for a better world and those who have lost hope;*

Know that the way we behave toward one another and toward other people is the fullest expression of what we believe;

Find more grace in the search for understanding than we do in dogmatic certainty, more value in questioning than in absolutes;

Form ourselves into communities dedicated to equipping one another for the work we feel called to do: striving for peace and justice among all people; protecting and restoring the integrity of all God's creation; and bringing hope to those Jesus called the least of his sisters and brothers;

Recognise that being followers of Jesus is costly, and entails selfless love, conscientious resistance to evil, and renunciation of privilege.

For information, please see our website, **www.pcnbritain.org.uk** or contact **info@pcnbritain.org.uk;**
St Faith's Vicarage, 62 Red Post Hill, London SE24 9JQ.

PCN – Britain is a registered charity, number 1102164.

 **THE SIBYLS**

Christian Spirituality Group for Transgender People
Write to BM Sibyls, London, WC1N 3XX
www.sibyls.co.uk

The Sibyls is a UK based confidential Christian spirituality group for transgender people, and their supporters, offering companionship along the journey, and information/advocacy to churches. Sibyls pray, eat, and talk together, and seek to fulfil Christ's command to love one another.

To keep members in touch with each other so that love and support may grow Sibyls provide:

- A newsletter
- Meetings, which include an act of worship
- A members' contact system
- A Yahoo group
- Some Sibyls speak to churches, employers and other organisations about being transgender.
- Members arrive at differing solutions to being transgender, and hold varying beliefs in matters of faith, religion and denomination.
- There are two important rules for members:
- To respect the security of each and every member, and never jeopardise it.
- To accept that other people's views are sincerely held and deserving of respect.

Partners are welcome at Sibyls' meetings, which always include serious matters and social time – prayer and a meal - and there are regular small gatherings throughout the year, in the country and in London. At major meetings a communion service is held. Many members are unable to find a church that will accept them as they are, or they are unable to attend communion as themselves.

Residential weekends, which take place twice yearly in the north and south of England, offer space and time to explore our ideas together, usually with a guest speaker, and for self discovery.

Continually exploring new ways and ideas, Sibyls is experienced based, i.e. it is assumed that belief arises from members' personal experience. Although essentially Christian, Sibyls is not preoccupied with church rules or dogmas, and firmly believes that transgender people are acceptable to God and part of God's purpose.

Student Christian Movement
Exploring together a radical faith

SCM is a movement seeking to bring together students of all backgrounds to explore the Christian faith in an open-minded and non-judgemental environment.

SCM seeks to promote a vision of Christianity that is:

inclusive
All people are welcome because our diversity is a gift to be celebrated.

aware
We recognise the importance of respect for and openness to other faiths.

radical
Faith and social justice cannot be separated.

challenging
Thinking through and questioning our faith ensures that it remains alive and dynamic.

We offer:
community
Student groups and **affiliated chaplaincies** *at over 60 colleges and universities and a large network of* **individual members** *and friends of all ages.*

events
Regular national events including **termly gatherings** *and an* **annual conference**

publications
Movement *magazine is published termly, and our* **publications** *are well known for their high quality and readability.*

international networks
Affiliated to the **World Student Christian Federation,** *providing members with the opportunity to participate in* **international conferences.**

To find out more, please contact us at:

SCM, 308F The Big Peg, 120 Vyse Street, Hockley, Birmingham B18 6ND
0121 200 3355 :: scm@movement.org.uk :: www.movement.org.uk

54

WATCH (Women and the Church) is campaigning
to see women take their place alongside men as bishops
and at every level in the Church of England

WATCH (Women and the Church)

WATCH has a vision of the Church of England as a community of God's people where regardless of their gender, justice and equality prevail. WATCH believes that this vision is rooted in the Scriptures and enfolds God's will for the whole world.

To realise this vision WATCH promotes:

- an enthusiasm for authentic equality of all people as a fundamental expression of the Gospel
- an inclusive ministry of women and men, lay and ordained, in the Church of England
- justice and the ending of discrimination against women in the Church of England
- honesty and openness in all appointments, so that women will have equal access to senior positions
- the appointment of women as bishops
- support for women in ministry, especially for those who encounter non-acceptance, resistance, obstruction or opposition at parochial or diocesan level and support for all those who suffer because of their advocacy of women's ministry
- a positive attitude to issues such as a renewed concept of God, collaborative working, inclusive language, questions of sexuality and education in these matters inside and outside the Church
- an understanding of a collaborative Church as an opportunity for growth and change for God's people rather than as a reason for fear
- theological study of all these issues
- the monitoring of the current deployment of women in ministry and the provision of an information service.

These aims and objectives are pursued in co operation (where appropriate) with other Anglican Churches, other Denominations and other organisations, such as GRAS(Group for Rescinding the Act of Synod), website: www.gras.org.uk.

Website: http://www.watchwomen.com
Address: St John's Church, Waterloo Road, London SE1 8TY

Wild Goose Publications is.... the publishing house of the Iona Community established in the Celtic Christian tradition of St Columba. We publish books and CDs on holistic spirituality, social justice, political and peace issues, healing, innovative approaches to worship, song and material for meditation and reflection.

Praying for the Dawn
A Resource Book for the Ministry of Healing
Ruth Burgess & Kathy Galloway
978 1 901557 26 8

Wild Goose Chase
Exploring the spirituality of everyday life
Annie Heppenstall
978 1 901557 95 7

Doing December Differently
an Alternative Christmas Handbook
Rosie Miles & Nicola Slee
978 1 905010 23 3

Gathered and Scattered
Readings and Meditation from the Iona Communit
Neil Paynter
978 1 901557 34 9

The Singing Thing Too
Enabling Congregations to Sing
John L Bell
978 1 905010 32 5

Stages on the Way
Worship Resources for Lent, Ho Week and Easter
Wild Goose Worship Group
978 1 901557 11 4

Fire and Bread
Resources from Easter Day to Trinity Sunday
Ruth Burgess
978 1 905010 30 1

Thinking Out Loud
Collected scripts from Rac 4's 'Thought for the Day'
John L Bell
978 1 905010 41 7

Love and Anger
Songs of lively faith and social justice
John L Bell & Graham Maule
978 0 947988 98 2

We Walk His Way
Shorter songs for worship
John L Bell
978 1 905010 55 4

Pearls of Life
For the personal spiritual journey
Lonnebo, Welin and Johansson
978 1 905010 39 4

Log on to www.ionabooks.com to browse our full list of publications, or alternatively contact Lorna on 0141 332 6292 or e-mail lorna@ionabooks.com to request a seasonal catalogue.

Wild Goose Publications is the publishing house of the Iona Community, a charity registered in Scotland No SC003794.

of God as 'the name we use for "isness without limitations," "isness" without limits'. To be Christian is to see Isness through the Christian lens of bible and Jesus. 'The question of God is not the question "Is there another being, a supreme being, in addition to the universe?" It is the question of how you are going to name, how you are going to see, "isness."

And we need also, in the process of shedding things, to lose our elevation and adulation of the ordained priesthood, which has disabled and devalued the majority of the members of church for centuries. One of us has struggled for over thirty years to escape the dangerous myth of church being that into which the ordained 'go'—somewhere they were not before, and somewhere other members of church apparently cannot be. Ordained priesthood has hijacked the true and primary priesthood of all Christian people. We need to recover a much more modest understanding of ordained priesthood as that of supporting and enabling the priestly gifts of all people to flourish and grow.

And what must we hold on to and develop? We must continue to tell the story of Jesus, while telling it in new ways. And we must continue to tell, as the heart of that story, of his extraordinary dream of the coming of God's kingdom on earth. The story is a way of life which affects how we work, how we treat one another, our family life, our political engagement and our stewardship—everything. Hope for the twenty-first Century—as well as hope for church in it—means ensuring that this is shared and owned by all of God's people, in all that we are and we do. To quote one of the Eight Points of progressive Christianity: 'we are people who form ourselves into communities dedicated to equipping one another for the work we feel called to do: striving for peace and justice among all people; protecting and restoring the integrity of all God's creation; and bringing hope to those Jesus called the least of his sisters and brothers.'

And then we need to rediscover the significance of symbols and myths as the way into what is 'true'. The story does not have to be read as history for it to be lived as truth. Indeed it will be better lived, and by more people, when the question 'Did it really happen?' gives ground to 'Can it be true?' Words cannot answer that question. But life shared with generosity, and offered freely to all, that can. Church is a eucharistic community, a thankful community, in that modest way of living. The Eucharist is the place of re-membering; the core place of gathering which nurtures and sustains, and then releases people into a life of love.

To be that generous release of love promises life and hope in plenty for the church, as both local and associational, in the twenty-first century. We just need to let the bird fly free.

"Bell and book and candle
cannot hold him any more,
for the bird is flying
as he did before."

Jill Sandham & Hugh Dawes

For reflection and discussion

What for you are the necessary elements of 'being church', from our history and in the present?

Which symbols and words reflect 'being church' – and which can be obstructive – in continuing to tell the story of Jesus?

By whose authority? What do you understand by 'authority' in the context of being church? And how, in practical terms, could current models of structure and authority change to reflect the way of Jesus in the institutional church?

Unity and diversity. What new ways can we find to work at this tension, locally and institutionally?

What are your personal hopes - for church, and for the church - in the 21st century?

For further reading

Marcus J.Borg, The Heart of Christianity, Harper Collins ISBN 0060730684

Hal Taussig, A New Spiritual Home, Polebridge Press ISBN 0944344712 (An analysis of progressive churches in the USA but with relevance for our situation in the UK)

Gordon Lynch, The New Spirituality, I.B. Tauris ISBN 1845114140 (A similar subject to Taussig but in the UK context)

John Shelby Spong, A New Christianity for a New World, Harper Collins ISBN 0060670630 (especially chapter 12)

Rowan Williams, Mission Shaped Church, Church House Publishing, ISBN 0715140132

John M. Hull, Mission-shaped Church: A Theological Response, SCM Press, ISBN 0334040574

Stuart Murray, Church after Christendom, Paternoster Press, ISBN 1842272926

Jack Good, The Dishonest Church, Rising Star Press ISBN 0933670095 (An American publication, now out of print but worth trying to get a second hand copy)

Finding Hope in the Modern World

Jonathan Clatworthy is an Anglican priest and General Secretary of the Modern Churchpeople's Union

We seem to be living in a time of deep changes—to our attitudes, our values and our hopes. It is as though the modern society which once gave us hope now increasingly looks like a dead end. Even our science and technology are under increasing attack.

These hopes and values have a history. The Black Death coincided with a time of rapidly developing technology. On the one hand anybody at all could be dead next week; on the other, human ingenuity seemed remarkably capable of devising new solutions to old hardships. A mood developed, best expressed by Francis Bacon who believed that nature is fallen—because Adam ate the apple—but God has given us science and technology to control it. The project of developing technology to control nature is still very much with us, but is now increasingly questioned.

Europeans have invested much hope in progress. Often it has been sought through other means; after the Second World War, for example, the victors hoped to create a better international order through political and economic structures like United Nations, the Common Market (now the EU) and the welfare state. More recently, though, political structures have lost prestige and our main symbols of progress have in effect been reduced to two: economic growth and new technologies. Immediately after the Second World War both were of great value. Today they are often tyrants. We do too much producing, too much buying, too much consuming, too much travelling. Since the late 1960s we have been increasingly aware of environmental damage: climate change, acid rain, ozone holes, pollution, soil erosion and extinctions. Social statistics, though they can always be disputed, do indicate that people today suffer more stress and mental illness than our predecessors a generation ago. Life expectancy is more likely to decline than rise as junk food, over-consuming and lack of exercise make us less healthy. Evolution did not design our bodies for the way we live.

Reactions to modernity

So many react against it. Some seek a simpler lifestyle. Others despise modern medicine and turn to eastern or pre-modern traditions instead. Postmodern culture characteristically abandons all hope of progress, insisting that there is nothing to hope for because we are not going anywhere in particular.

Religion is playing its part. A precursor was Karl Barth, who argued that when we read in the Bible about things which do not fit modern science, it should be the Bible which judges modern beliefs, not the other way round. God is free to break the laws of nature and perform miracles.[1] More recently many 'conservative' postmodern theologians[2] have appealed to their preferred authority—the Bible or the Church or first century Christianity—as something which stands over against modern society, passing judgement on it, in much the same way as religious opposition to evolution presents fundamentalist Christianity as an alternative to modern science. We are offered only two options: either to accept modernity as a complete self-contained package, together with its drive for ever-increasing production and consumption, and a blind faith in technology as a solution to all its problems; or to reject it in its entirety, seeking a return to some past golden age free of everything modern.

Biblical support for science and technology

Against these back-to-the-past proposals I shall defend modernity's vision of hope for the future in two ways. Modernity's view of knowledge and progress, far from recommending a single self-contained lifestyle, provides the means for self-criticism and change. First, though, I shall argue that modernity's affirmation of science and technology is rooted in biblical values. I offer four illustrations.

---

1 Hunsinger, George, *How to Read Karl Barth: The Shape of his Theology*, Oxford: OUP, 1991, pp.34, 51 & 289 n.1.

2 Thus John Milbank prioritizes the Church, as he understands it, as the lens through which Christians should interpret everything else, and Richard Hays argues that 'the world narrated by the New Testament witnesses' should be the basis of our understanding of reality. Milbank, John, *Theology and Social Theory: Beyond Secular Reason*, Oxford: Blackwells, 1990, p.388 (see also pp.246 & 387); Hays, RB, *The Moral Vision of the New Testament*: HarperCollins/T&TClark, 1996, p.296.

1 Regularity All science has to presuppose that the world operates regularly enough to be understood. This is not self-evident: it is equally possible either to believe that the world is basically chaotic, and try to explain away the apparent regularities, or to believe that the world is basically ordered and try to explain away the apparent irregularities.

Ancient polytheists generally preferred the first option: the forces of nature operated unpredictably, according to the decisions of self-willed gods, so science could not develop. Some ancient Greek philosophers, however, proposed the idea of regular, predictable laws of nature. On its own this idea only claims that there are regularities, without establishing their cause or their scope. Another tradition, Judaism, made a different contribution based on its monotheism. The Jewish scriptures describe the world as designed by a single benevolent being who intended it for the well-being of all creation and got it right. This view provides a conceptual framework for expecting the world to be ordered rather than chaotic. God intends *shalom* - peace, harmony, well-being and prosperity, for humans, animals and the land.

Order and regularity are not quite the same thing. Basil of Caesarea, a fourth century Christian bishop, combined these two notions - to the satisfaction of European scientists for well over a thousand years - by incorporating the Greek notion of laws of nature *within* the Jewish-Christian notion of creation by God, and thus explained regularity as an intended aspect of the created order.

2 Comprehensibility For science to be possible it was also necessary to believe that the human mind is capable of understanding that order. On what basis might we expect to have this capacity? According to Basil, the same God had created the laws of nature to be regular and the human mind to understand them. The two were part of the same design.

Closely linked with this was Basil's notion of the *relative autonomy* of nature. This is an intermediate position between two extremes. One extreme proposes that the physical universe is completely dependent on divine initiatives, so we cannot predict anything. This makes science impossible. The other extreme is the determinist theory that every event is caused by previous events in an unfailing sequence, so that the entire future of the universe is predetermined and there is no such thing as human free will. This also makes science impossible, because if all our thoughts are determined by physical causes we have no reason to suppose that any of them are true. Basil's monotheist Christian cosmology could defend relative autonomy by proposing that the laws of nature operated reliably but only within the bounds set by a God of goodness.

3 Technology With respect to technology one single biblical text has dominated the debate:

God created humankind in his image, in the image of God he created them; male and female he created them. God blessed them, and God said to them, 'be fruitful and multiply, and fill the earth and subdue it; and have dominion over the fish of the sea and over the birds of the air and over every living thing that moves upon the earth. (Genesis 1:27-28)

This has often been cited to argue that God has given humans permission to do what they like with non-human nature, without concern for its own well-being. The authors of the text cannot have meant any such thing. They knew nothing of modern technological practices. They did, however, know of the contentious new technologies of their own day, tilling the ground and domesticating cattle. Did these activities make God angry? The authors of this text assert that they did not. They did not, however, give them *carte blanche*: they were well aware of the great many laws, listed elsewhere in the Bible, which limited what farmers might do with their animals and fields. The text, in other words, *affirmed* the use of those technologies but still expected their use to be limited. Technology was to be used not for its own sake but for the sake of *shalom*.

4 Evil spirits Some western churches have 'rediscovered' evil spirits as 'biblical', and developed ministries of exorcism accordingly. This is a misunderstanding of the ancient situation. Evil spirits were certainly a popular theme with Mark who described six exorcisms, and Matthew and Luke copied him. Far more significant, however, is the fact that there is no mention of evil spirits anywhere in the Old Testament, precisely because of the Jewish commitment to monotheism. This is a most remarkable witness to consistent editing, since throughout the rest of the ancient near east evil spirits were taken for granted as ubiquitous; generally, they were blamed for all illness. For Christians today to affirm their existence as 'biblical' is, therefore, to side with Mark and the pagans *against* the bulk of the Bible.

The issue became significant in the early stages of modern science. Medieval folklore assumed that invisible spirits abounded, capable of making changes to the physical world. This meant there could be no predictability, no regularity in nature, and therefore no science. Early modern scientists therefore rejected this view, rigidly separating the spiritual from the physical, treating all physical things as observable and spiritual things as unobservable. It was an over-reaction, though necessary if science was to be possible.

For these four reasons, therefore, I believe we should not describe modernity with its science and technology as hostile to the biblical tradition. On the contrary it would be more accurate to describe it as a legitimate development of it; it is the anti-scientific reactions, like the idea that God put the fossils in the rocks 6,000 years ago and the revival of exorcisms, which are theologically closest to the ancient polytheism which the biblical authors rejected.

Progress

What ground does this give us for hope in the modern world? We cannot have hope without a sense of progress, and we cannot have progress without a sense of purpose—objectives which we are trying to reach.

Again biblical monotheism offers distinctive possibilities. Historians of progress have described how the ancient world knew a variety of theories about world history. One was that history goes round in circles, so that whatever happens will happen again, perhaps thousands of years in the future. Another was alternation between a golden age and a dark age, and another again was gradual deterioration from better ages to worse ones.

Judaism offered a more positive alternative: the idea of *linear* development, a gradual process of change from the past to the future with the possibility of long-term improvement. It is perhaps best expressed by the Old Testament prophets as they describe the history of Israel and urge the nation to adopt particular courses of action for the sake of a better future. The picture of history they have bequeathed to us has the following elements. Firstly, the idea of *purpose*. Because they (or the editors of their prophecies) believed God had designed the people for *shalom*, there was a long-term vision, a future to strive towards. Secondly, the idea of *progress* towards the goal: small successes can help towards the long-term goal. Thirdly, the idea of *interrupted* progress. Sometimes we do the wrong thing, or events take an unfortunate turn; we go three steps forward and two steps back. Fourthly, the idea of *hope*. Even when circumstances are absolutely dire and we cannot see any possibility of improvement, we accept that our own understanding of the situation is only partial and in the greater scheme of things progress remains a possibility.

These concepts of purpose, progress and hope are not inevitable. Just as in the ancient world there were alternative views of history which had no place for them, so also some recent attacks on modernity also reject them. An example is Thomas Kühn's theory about science. Modernism generally sees science as gradually progressing, with each generation building on the discoveries of its predecessors. Kühn's theory opens up the possibility that instead it alternates;

usually it builds on the inherited scientific paradigm, but sometimes it jumps rather quickly to a different paradigm, thus making long-term progress impossible. Similarly commentators on postmodern culture describe it as abandoning any sense of long-term objectives, let alone progress towards them.

Let us then apply these concepts of purpose, progress and hope to the current controversies about modernity.

Firstly, they rule out the possibility of reverting to a past golden age. There never was one, and in any case we cannot return exactly to a particular point in the past.

Secondly, if there is to be hope for progress we must value what is good about the tradition we have inherited. Progress takes place when we discover, within the resources available to us, the potential for future development. So the science and technology which have provided many welcome products, but at the expense of generating global warming, can also warn us about it and help us find ways to respond to it.

Thirdly, if true progress is towards the ultimate purposes for which God has designed us—that *shalom* which we only ever experience in part—all the tools we use to aspire towards it, whether political institutions like the United Nations, or economic growth, or scientific knowledge or technological innovation, are, and must be seen as, only tools. They are not ends in themselves. Like everything God enables us to do, they have potential for good but also potential for harm. Our task is to affirm them but limit them.

Contrary to those who despise the present and long to return to some past age, it is 'Enlightenment reason' with its commitment to open debate and critical analysis which keeps modern thought open-ended, willing to take on board new insights, admit its mistakes and change direction. Just as democracy enables voters to opt for different political priorities, so also the sciences which made western consumerist society possible can also warn us against its excesses and open up alternative possibilities. Modernity, rather than being one of two options, provides a basis for choosing between many different options.

Christians, therefore, instead of looking backwards, can instead affirm our own time and place as part of a living, developing tradition. All living traditions have a story to tell about their origins, and in the same way Christians value the insights of the Bible—not because we preserve them unaltered, but because we find them *fruitful*. Progress takes place when we value what our predecessors have achieved and find in their achievements the tools for greater achievements still. When modernity expresses positive hopes for the future, it stands in a long tradition, Christian and biblical.

Jonathan Clatworth

For reflection and discussion

What do you hope the world will be like for your family in 50 years' time? In 100 years' time?

Do you think society makes progress? In what ways is our society better than it was in the past?

If it is possible to make the world a better place, what are the most important contributors? Science? Technology? Politics? Economics? Morality? Anything else?

How do we assess the benefits and costs of particular technological innovations—for example,

Biofuels. Do they help reduce the use of oil, or push food prices up because of the land they use, or maintain an obsession with mass travel which needs to be questioned?

Research on human embryos and human/animal combinations. Does it contravene the principle of the sanctity of life, or affirm it by producing new possibilities for medical treatment?

Military technology. Do bigger and better bombs constitute progress or regress? Or does it all depend on who possesses them?

For further reading

Ian Barbour, Religion and Science: Historical and Contemporary Issues, SCM Press 0334027217

Jonathan Clatworthy, Liberal Faith in a Divided Church: O Books, ISBN 1846941164

Richard Holloway, Godless Morality, Canongate Books, ISBN 1841955787

Keith Ward, God, Chance & Necessity, One World Publications ISBN , 1851681167

John MacDonald Smith, Understanding God's World: Models in Theology and Science, MCU Forewords, available from the MCU office (See directory page)

"Out of Eden":
The Hope for Women and Men in Christ

Christina Rees is Chair of WATCH
(Women and the Church)

Imagine, if you will, Adam and Eve in the Garden, but imagine that there is no threat to come of the beguiling snake or of the apple, taken and eaten. Imagine, too, that there will be no need for the fig leaves. Picture instead the man and the woman, standing together, side by side, surrounded by the beauty of creation.

It is hard for us to think what relationships between women and men would be like without the effects of fear, hatred, scorn, disgust, humiliation, resentment, envy and domination. It is hard to imagine a world without sin and without pain.

But I believe that is just what we need to be imagining, because I believe that the unequal and distorted relationships between men and women are as much part of the brokenness of the world as is all other evil and cruelty. The fallenness of the world includes the fractured harmony between the sexes. I believe that God intended that all humanity and all creation should exist in a state such as the *shalom* of Isaiah's shining vision, in which swords are re-fashioned into ploughs for tilling the soil and spears into hooks for pruning trees.

Isaiah's *shalom* implies not only the cessation of war and violence, but also the existence of security, abundance, joy ... 'and sorrow and sighing shall flee away'. (Is 35:10) But that vision is hard to hold: we have eaten of the tree of the knowledge of good and evil and there is no going back. We are aware of our nakedness, and our hearts ache within us. We look at one another through the shadows of mistrust and suspicion. We look at ourselves with disappointment and self-loathing. We cannot keep hold of any peace, our sense of living an abundant life is pale and fleeting, and all the sweetness has gone. We realise we have lost our way and we long for something more.

Now, imagine the Cross. On the rough-hewn beams, Jesus' body hangs heavily. His breath is weakening, but before he dies, he shouts out the words "It is finished!" What, what is finished?

What are we to make of the Cross? For most of the time, between then and now, even in the darkest and most painful of times, millions of people around the world have spoken the steady words: "I believe in the forgiveness of sins, the resurrection of the body and the life everlasting".

The Cross remains a mystery, a scandal, an outrage, a miscarriage of justice. We also believe it to be a divine transaction, the means of salvation, the key to the turning point of all of hope and life. The Cross will always lie beyond our full comprehension and only ever be even partly understood, yet we have faith that it has made all the difference in the world. And those of us who have only heard the stories, who were not there to betray, deny or mourn our Lord, approach the Cross by walking backwards from the Resurrection, and because of that we walk in hope: what was impossible is now possible, what could not be now is. "All shall be well," said Mother Julian, and in the eternal Now, we believe, all *is* well.

Thundering over the centuries and exploding into the lives of those who have ears to hear, let us receive the proclamation of truth and hope written by Saint Paul, a man who hung all his hope on the truth of the Risen Christ and the power of the Resurrection: "There is therefore now no condemnation for those who are in Christ Jesus. For the law of the Spirit of life in Christ Jesus has set me free from the law of sin and death", and "if the Spirit of him who raised Jesus from the dead dwells in you, he who raised Christ Jesus from the dead will give life to your mortal bodies also through his Spirit which dwells in you." (Romans 8:1-2, 11)

Do we dare to hope? Can it be true that because of what Jesus accomplished on the Cross and because of the empty tomb the effects of sin can be undone, obliterated, annihilated? Is there a way back to the Garden?

We may still long for it, and sometimes think we can remember the scent of its flowers, but I do not think the Garden exists any more. When the man and the woman left, it grew tangled and wild, then dry and barren, and the path was lost and forgotten. Reclaiming innocence is not possible, but there is another way.

When Jesus first started to preach, testing his wild vision on his friends, he told them to imagine, not a garden, but a kingdom, a strange, unlikely kingdom, peopled by strange and unlikely citizens: those who know they are spiritually poor, those who mourn, the humble, the merciful, the pure in heart, those who work for peace and those whose greatest desire is to do what God requires, even if they are persecuted for it.

Imagine this kingdom, Jesus said, because it is already here among you, and if you love and long for this kingdom, it will grow bigger and stronger and even more beautiful. It will be for all those who believe in it a new way, and within its walls will be found wholeness, peace, *shalom*.

In this kingdom women and men greet one another as equals, they bow in respect when they meet, and embrace as sisters and brothers. When one of them is praised, they all celebrate; when one of them suffers, they are all filled with sorrow. Everyone is the same height, so that when they come face to face they can look each other straight in the eye, and their eyes are like crystals, shining with clear, dancing light, in all the colours of the seas and the skies and the stones and the earth.

As they enter the kingdom each one is given a box, an ornate treasure chest, with their name engraved in gold on it. They are also given a key, and told that whatever they find in the box is theirs, to be taken and used for the good of all, and enjoyed. When they open the boxes they find exquisite jewels and clothing; no two boxes hold the same treasure. As the people go about their working and living, each of them wears their own fine clothes, their own precious jewels, and they delight in each other's unique splendour and beauty.

I believe that in the kingdom of God, here among us now, there is no rule of patriarchy, no privileging of males over females.

I believe that women are made in the image of God as are men, in their bodies as well as in their minds and their spirits.

I believe that God embraces the feminine as much as God embraces the masculine.

I believe that the significance of the Incarnation is about God becoming human, sharing in the life and experience of all humanity, men and women and children.

In the Kingdom of God here among us now, we can resist the deceit of idolatry, of creating an image of God in our own image, of picturing God as male. As Jesus said to the thirsty woman at the well, as they spoke together in the heat and dust, "God is spirit, and only by the power of his spirit can people worship him as he really is." When we look at Jesus we see God, but not God in the maleness, but God in the humanity, in the compassion, the faithfulness, the truth and integrity of action and word.

When Moses came down from the mountain with the tablets of stone, he warned the Israelites that it was idolatry to worship any gods other than the one true God. Today, we acknowledge our worship of many other gods, including the god of maleness: male power, male reason and male strength. Throughout Christian history, some theologians, wise in other ways, but blind to their own idolatry, have written and spoken of a god in whom the feminine has no part, and whose image cannot be seen in the bodies of women. Revered teachers and learned scholars have repeatedly insisted that in the Divine there is no room for the feminine. In the middle of the nineteenth century, a Swiss historian called Bachofen seemed to sum up this entire body of thought when he declared that human development is only finished when it has succeeded in liberating itself from any connection with the female: "the feminine principle is in the way to our rise to immortality."

It was believed by Aristotle, and by those who came after him, nearly up to the time of the Enlightenment, that the male seed contained all that was necessary to form new life: the woman was just the incubator. Further, it was believed that all humans would be born male, and that it was only when the woman got caught in an east wind, or sat on a damp patch of ground, that babies were then born female. The Christian philosopher, Thomas Aquinas, considered women to be 'misbegotten males'. He also believed that when men failed in this life, they would be reincarnated as women: when women failed, they would come back as beasts.

Holy, educated, Christian men of their day pronounced variously that women were the 'devil's gateway' (Tertullian), or that 'woman is a temple built over a sewer' (Jerome), or opined that 'to embrace a woman is to embrace a sack of manure' (Odo of Cluny).

Even the great Augustine wrestled with how to consider women, especially in relation to God. Augustine was a man tortured by a strong sexual drive, whose understanding of sexuality and of women caused him, ultimately, to reject the love of his life. However, in spite of, and possibly because of, his own personal torment, Augustine painstakingly worked out a way of thinking about women that was actually an improvement on what his contemporaries thought. Augustine bravely argued that it was possible for women to bear the image of God, but only in their minds, and not, as he agreed with his colleagues, in their bodies. There could be nothing of the image of the Divine in women's bodies, as there was, of course, in males' bodies.

Human history, including Christian history, has not been neutral for women. Whether it was as a result of faulty scientific knowledge, or customs and traditions, fear and ignorance, throughout the centuries women have been beaten, bound, burned, constrained, imprisoned, mutilated, violated and killed—for being female or for posing a threat to the male-defined orthodoxy. Women have been told who they are, what they want, what they are capable of, what to do, what they cannot do, what to think and what not to think for as long as history records the writings and interactions of humankind.

We would be foolish to think that the legacy of this grievous past has faded away. We still see the persistence of patriarchy when we witness today men defining and proscribing the lives of women, in both secular and religious institutions and in societies across the world. In some Anglican Churches women are still told that they are not capable of being priests, that ordination does not 'take' on female flesh. In the Roman Catholic Church it is officially forbidden even to discuss the ordination of women. Malignant remnants of the past still cast their shadows today in the cutting, raping and murdering of wives, daughters and sisters for the sake of doctrines and creeds written and interpreted by men.

It is time to walk away from human sin and evil, time to breathe again the reviving air of the vision of Isaiah. Do we believe? Do we believe that, in spite of everything, including our individual and collective complacency and complicity, that shalom, even shalom between women and men is possible?

Do we believe in what happened to Saint Paul, a man whose lust and zeal for killing Christians was replaced with a vision of risen Christ and of the love of God so powerful that it sustained him all the way through persecutions, storms and imprisonment, all the way to the executioner's block? "I count everything as loss," he declared to the believers at Philippi, "because of the surpassing worth of knowing Christ Jesus my Lord."

Do we believe with Paul that, for those who have been baptised into Christ, all that might create divisions and barriers between us has been torn down, including our ethnicity, wealth and sex? Do we believe that when God's Spirit pours out gifts, that the outpouring is dependent on the openness of our hearts and the uniqueness of our persons and not on whether we happen to be male or female?

Do we believe that for those who are in Christ, the old way of being and seeing really has passed away and that there is a whole new way of being and seeing opened to us? Do we believe that God really is going about the business of drawing the whole world back to into the heart of the Divine—liberating, transforming, reconciling all people for the sake of the ultimate unity of all creation?

If we claim our full inheritance in Christ, then we will stand against division and domination, we will refuse the temptations to faction or fraction. We will recognise and honour God's image in one another, and we will live and work and minister as equals, male and female together.

On the night he was betrayed, Jesus prayed one of his last earthly prayers. He prayed that all those who believed in him would be united in love in the same way in which he was united with God, in a love so vivid and real that it would persuade all others of the truth of the Good News and of the reality and unity of the Sender and the One who had been sent. Ultimately, the hope of inclusion is not only for women and men, but for all of creation, but until and unless we can accept that we are all one in Christ, freed to be who God has called us to be, then we will continue to struggle and long for the greater *shalom*.

Christina Rees

For reflection and discussion

In the closing paragraphs of this chapter, Christina Rees asks the reader a number of challenging questions. What is your response?

For further reading

For further information about women's ordination and the Church of England:

Harriet Harris and Jane Shaw, The Call for Women Bishops, SPCK Publishing, ISBN 0281056218

Women and the Episcopate, Affirming Catholicism, Journal 2006.

For books of Christian feminist theology:

Ann Loades and Karen Armstrong, Feminist Theology, A Reader, Westminster/John Knox Press, U.S. ISBN 0664251293

Elisabeth Schussler Fiorenza, Sharing Her Word: Feminist Biblical Interpretation in Context, T and T Clark Ltd ISBN 0567086488

Rosemary Radford Ruether, Feminist Theologies: Legacy and Prospect, Augsburg Fortress, ISBN 0800638948

Hope for the Poorest
of the World

Dr. Paula Clifford is Head of
Theology at Christian Aid and
the Archbishop of Canterbury's
Advisor on Climate Change

Jesus unrolled the scroll and found the place where it was written.
The Spirit of the Lord is upon me,
because he has anointed me
to bring good news to the poor ...
And he rolled up the scroll ... and began to say to them
'Today this scripture has been fulfilled in your hearing.'
(Luke 4:17-18, 21, quoting Isaiah 61)

1. The biblical basis

The Gospels show us that Jesus was indeed deeply concerned for people who were poor or in some way on the fringes of society. He associated freely and often with the marginalised—'tax collectors and sinners'—and welcomed the company of women and children, and others held in low esteem in the culture of his day. They were the object of many of his healing miracles, and they took their place among his followers.

The many actions of Jesus that are in themselves 'good news for the poor' are of course an example that we as Christians are called to follow as best we can. And the prophecy that he read in the Nazareth synagogue is an early indication of what that might mean.

Those verses from Isaiah are a central part of so-called 'Trito-(or Third) Isaiah'—chapters 56 to 65 of the Old Testament book we know simply as Isaiah—written in the years following the return of a small number of Jewish exiles from Babylon. And they are a reminder that this homecoming was not the great moment of salvation that people had hoped for.

The first returnees were a wretched bunch. All that awaited them was devastation: no infrastructure, no social, political or religious structures. Furthermore, they were disillusioned and guilt-ridden, their predicament a direct result of their forebears' unfaithfulness to the God of Israel.

So the task of Third Isaiah is to address a demoralised people and to reassure them of salvation in the future. And that is the Christian calling as well: not only to care for people who are self-evidently suffering physically or mentally, but also to address the underlying needs of those who, like the returning exiles, are quite simply disillusioned, the victims of other people's actions.

Isaiah 61 also demonstrates that the prophet himself is a mouthpiece, a mediator of God's word, bringing good news to the poor. It is not the prophet who sets the captives free and binds up the broken-hearted. That falls to the people who hear and respond to the prophetic voice. So Jesus fulfils Isaiah's prophecy in his teaching (his prophetic voice), calling his followers to active service of those in need, to follow his own unparalleled example of compassion and healing for people who are in any kind of need, visible or not. It is for us now to respond.

2. Theology in action

It is telling that Isaiah 61/Luke 4 speaks of oppression (the prophet is anointed 'to let the oppressed go free'), because oppression is a sign of injustice. And injustice—the systematic failure to love our neighbour as ourselves—is the root cause of much suffering in many different forms. Throughout the Bible there is the command to shun injustice, from Micah's call to 'do justice, and to love kindness', to Paul's comment on the command of Jesus, 'Love does no wrong to a neighbour; therefore, love is the fulfilling of the law'. (Romans 13:10)

The message of Isaiah 61, renewed by Jesus in Luke 4, is a call to all of us to address suffering and oppression, and to recognise that these may take many different forms. In other words, *we* are the source of hope for the poorest people. It is not something we can hand over without question to government or to 'the church': hope lies in us and in what we are prepared to do.

Yet a realistic response to poverty, whether in first-century Palestine or in today's global village, cannot be based on an individualist, piecemeal approach. That was not the way of Jesus who commanded his disciples to go and make disciples of the nations: not just here and there, but *all* nations. A realistic approach to poverty is not to patch up the bits you can see: it depends on uncovering its causes. And when we consider the suffering of poor people in the face of HIV and AIDS, climate change, civil war or even natural disasters, identifying and remedying the underlying injustice is vitally important.

One example is the situation of women with HIV in countries where gender inequality is rife. There are countless stories of wives being blamed for their husband's infection and thrown out of their homes as a result. Marsilie, a former teacher living on the outskirts of Kinshasa in the Democratic Republic in Congo, is a case in point: 'My husband's family took away everything. I was left alone crying with my five children'. In this instance more is needed to address Marsilie's situation than simply providing food and medication. One of Christian Aid's partners in Kinshasa, an organisation called 'Fondation Femmes Plus', works to support HIV-positive women but crucially also to address the discrimination that is keeping them poor.

When disaster strikes it is the poorest people who suffer most. Several years after the Asian tsunami, poor fishermen in Tamil Nadu were still waiting for their government to decide where their replacement homes should be built. During the civil war in Burundi the poorest subsistence farmers had to leave their hillside homes as rebel and government troops battled in the hills and destroyed the forests that had also protected the farms.

The crisis of climate change reveals such injustice on a global scale. The major cause of global warming is CO_2 emissions by the richest countries of the world, yet the people who are already suffering and dying as a result are those who have done least to bring this situation about: the poorest people in some of the world's poorest countries. Rising sea levels in Bangladesh are driving poor people away from the coastal areas where they earn a living from fishing, while poor farmers in central America are unable to replace their crops and livestock lost to increasingly violent hurricanes. And this represents a double challenge: the injustice needs to be corrected by restoring the livelihoods that have been lost but also by enabling development to continue. In El Salvador, a poor farmer called Mauricio summed up the state of his community like this: 'Here we live off what we harvest, and the animals, but during Hurricane Stan [in 2005] we lost our cows. It takes five years to save enough money to replace a lost animal, so Stan was a disaster. This community has been here since 1993 and some people still don't have houses or latrines'.

If the message of Isaiah 61 and Luke 4 is one of hope for Marsilie and Mauricio, what exactly can they hope for?

Responding to suffering effectively is not an optional extra for the church. St Paul's picture in 1 Corinthians 12:26 of the church as the body of Christ brings this very close to home: 'if one member suffers, all suffer together with it'. In other words, however remote the need may appear, it is nonetheless owned by each one of us, and an appropriate response is demanded. Back in 2000, South African churches were distributing badges that read 'The body of Christ has AIDS'—a painful message, and one that is still not well understood in many parts of that worldwide body. Yet hope for the poorest depends on every part of the church feeling their suffering, making that suffering their own, and responding accordingly.

Hope for the poorest people, then, lies in our taking on their suffering as if it were our own or that of those dearest to us, living out to the full the command to love our neighbour as ourselves. The work of a Christian development agency in this context is twofold: to show people just who their neighbour is, and to advocate an appropriate response to that neighbour's needs.

3. Our response

Our Christian response to the suffering of the world's poorest people, whether as churches or as individuals, has to meet three basic criteria: it must be compassionate, proportionate and effective. Think of Jesus miraculously feeding the crowds who had gathered to listen to him. It all began because he had compassion on them after three days with nothing to eat (Mark 8:2). His response was in keeping with the size of the problem: he provided food for all of them. And it was effective—so much so that there were twelve baskets of food left over. We see the same pattern in his healing miracles: they begin with Jesus's compassion and there are no half measures in how he responds to people's needs.

(a) A compassionate response

Compassion is not just feeling sorry for someone. Compassion means taking on someone else's suffering. And that means understanding both the nature and the cause of that suffering. People often complain that it is difficult to pray for people and situations they don't know. True enough, but it is not hard to find out. So a compassionate response depends firstly on the will to look and listen, to search out details in the press or via the internet and to reflect on the specific forms of injustice that are keeping poor people poor.

A compassionate response is also a willing and unconditional response. Generosity is praised in the New Testament: Jesus singles out the gift of a poor widow to the Temple treasury (Luke 21:2-4) while, as Paul writes to Timothy, the rich are 'to do good, to be rich in good works, generous and ready to share' (1 Timothy 6:18). Yet how reluctant we are, by comparison, to give of our time, our talents or our wealth. People often say that they like to see where their money is going or to have some say on how it is spent—a far cry from the widow who unconditionally gave 'all that she had to live on'.

(b) A proportionate response

By any standards the behaviour of the poor widow was disproportionate. The Bible already sets high standards—the traditional tithe, giving away one-tenth of one's income, is a demanding discipline, yet one that needs to be viewed in the light of the sacrificial giving of Jesus. Our compassion, like his, should set new levels of generosity for the church and for ourselves. But it is also crucial that our response to the poorest people should be proportionate not just to our means but to their needs and to the causes of their needs.

The climate change crisis has highlighted these factors in a deeply uncomfortable way. The injustice of the way in which global warming is affecting the poorest people has so far failed to evoke a significant compassionate response from the churches, let alone one which is proportionate to the size of the problem. While people die or are driven from their homes as a result of extreme weather, we are content with worthy but barely significant activities (installing low-energy light bulbs or sharing electric mowers) or even irrelevant ones (42 per cent of us apparently believe that recycling our rubbish will combat climate change). The argument that if, say, everyone used trains and buses, things would change is unconvincing. There is little point in appealing to altruism in an essentially non-altruistic society.

A proportionate response to climate change lies elsewhere: in lobbying national and international bodies and demanding legislation that will force us to reduce our carbon emissions to a level that will seriously affect the lifestyles of all of us. We have to speak out and take action (Micah 6:8), and until the church faces up to the full implications of what it means to 'do justice' it cannot claim to offer a lead in protecting the earth and its people.

(c) An effective response

It follows from all this that the church's response to poverty has to be effective. There is no point in organising Synod debates or setting up committees if these are not followed up by real action. But I suggest that there are two key ways in which the church is uniquely placed to make an effective response.

The first suggestion is that the church should recover its calling to be a servant. The teaching of Jesus that 'the Son of Man came not to be served but to serve' is not always easy to discern within the church, which for some is a means of satisfying ambition and acquiring status. Liberation theology has shown us the way forward in empowering poor communities; but until it becomes the ambition of the churches in the North to stand together in an attitude of service with those in the South, our response to the poorest people cannot hope to be fully effective.

My second suggestion is that the church should recover its prophetic voice. Despite the growth of secularism, people nationally and internationally still want to hear the ethical voice and see the moral leadership of the churches. Yet all too often that voice is silent, or else shows little understanding of today's world. An effective response to the poor will reflect compassion and understanding, and in calling for action on the root causes of poverty and injustice it will deliver a clear message to the rich world.

Being a servant and being prophetic is not the prerogative of church leaders and people in power. It is also the calling of individual Christians in their different situations. For the church as an institution and all its members to speak out on behalf of the poor and to live in service to them would be a truly effective response to their needs.

Conclusion

Throughout the Bible, unsurprisingly, we encounter concern for those who suffer poverty and injustice. What is more surprising, and often overlooked, is how radical this message is when it comes to offering hope to those affected. Their suffering is to be our suffering; the voice of the prophets speaking out against injustice is to be our voice; Jesus's ministry of service to the poor is to be our ministry.

In the light of that, the mission of the churches and their members has to lie in a compassionate, effective and proportionate response to the needs of the poorest people. That is where their hope lies and where it must be fulfilled.

Paula Clifford, Christian Aid

For discussion

Nearly 190 countries have signed up to the Millennium Development Goals ('MDGs'), which were agreed at the United Nations Millennium Summit in September 2000. The first of them is to 'eradicate extreme poverty and hunger'. In July 2007, the UK Prime Minister Gordon Brown and the UN Secretary General Ban Ki-Moon launched the MDG call to action, which seeks to 'harness the efforts of every possible government, organisation, group and individual with a contribution to make'. How can the church best contribute to this process?

In what ways can individual Christians make a response to poverty that is compassionate, proportionate and effective?

For further reading

The issues raised in this chapter can be explored through visiting the websites of a number of development agencies, mission societies and other organisations. Resources, written and visual, abound and there is material for children and young peoples groups. These would include ~

Christian Aid - www.christian.org.uk

Oxfam - www.oxfam.org.uk

Tearfund - www.tearfund.org

World Development Movement - www.wdm.org.uk

Operation Noah - www.operationnoah.org

There is a climate change course for use in church groups - the Omega Climate Change Course - www.omegaclimate.org.uk

Recent books include ~

Robert Hensen, The Rough Guide to Climate Change, Rough Guides Limited, ISBN 1858281059

Nick Spencer and Robert White, Christianity, Climate Change and Sustainable Living, SPCK Publishing, ISBN 0281058334

Not so recent but well worth reading,

Michael Taylor, Christianity, Poverty and Wealth, SPCK, ISBN 0281055475

Michael Taylor, Poverty and Christianity, SCM Press, ISBN 0334028140

Singing in the Rain
The Hope of Inclusion

*Revd Clare Herbert is
Coordinator of Inclusive Church*

This chapter is about my acknowledgement that it is raining, inside, outside, all around me, and about my learning to sing in the rain, to transform the world around me by faith and hope.

The "rain" I describe is the sexual orientation known as lesbian or homosexual and its growing acceptance in our secular culture, recently demonstrated by the Civil Partnerships Act of 2004 and the Equality Act Regulations of 2007 from which some of us benefit. At a deeper level "the rain" is our starting to understand that homosexuality is part of us all, to be carefully considered and reflected over, rather than rejected and pushed away.

Acknowledging that it is raining, both within and without, appears to set people free to express the most ordinary desires—for companionship, laughter, feeding the cat, looking after children, leading choirs and planning day-care for elderly relatives. Gay and lesbian people are being accepted and challenged to lead "normal" lives within society and some choose to go to Church. At Church they may find it to display Gene Kelly's enthusiastic enjoyment of the rain!

Many members of the Church pretend that it is not raining, or not raining enough as to worry about. They disdain all open discussion of homosexuality, failing to understand that for gay and lesbian people accustomed to belong in a society which values equality and diversity such silence is incomprehensible and, for some, personally painful.

Other parts of the Church know that it is indeed raining so try to put the Church under a huge Centre-park roof so that they do not have to feel the rain. The dome consists of a condemnatory attitude towards all physical expression of homosexuality and is held up by strict adherence to certain biblical texts. Such energy is necessary to support this roof that little goes in to understanding gay and lesbian Christians suffering its weight.

Yet other parts of the Church do a sort of "war dance" in the rain, raising their umbrellas and chanting that everyone must enjoy the rain equally! While these parts of the Church provide a welcome temporary home for gay and lesbian Christians, and are particularly good at accepting their rage, they overlook the deep-felt longing in some to become integrated into a Church family rather than engaging long-term in a battle.

For most of us who are gay and lesbian Christians it is hard to find a place to sing and dance! But it is possible, singing in the rain, and important to grow in our awareness that we posses insights to share. We transform the world by the offer of our selves. The discovery of my own self, my own faith and hope, began with the discovery of a dance partner.

Faith sustained by dancing with "the other"

I grew up in an isolated part of North Devon, in the mid 1960s, where Church was community and the language of faith the language of life. Two degrees in theology and ordination training extended my knowledge of the Gospel. That is, I knew *the words* rather well—of love, salvation, forgiveness, new life—but I was dead inside. I had a sense of the centre of my body being shaped like a coffin. I knew from looking around me what the words of salvation should mean, but I didn't possess their meaning in any way which brought me joy and hope.

In my first job as a deaconess and university chaplain in Bristol I met Professor Dennis Nineham, and began to talk to him. He obviously thought I was far too churchy for my own good, far too ready to accept the undervaluing of women current in the employment practices of the Church, and suggested my giving the Church a break. As I struggled to see how I would survive he encouraged me to understand his view that theology needs a dancing partner to bring it to life. He believed I should not merely have a rest from Church but find the "dancing partner" with and against which to form my own theology.

Slowly this idea of life with the dancing partner began to take root. I changed my life-style, became a social worker and entered in to psychoanalysis. In psychoanalysis and psychodynamic counselling I found the dancing partner to theology for me which would eventually bring me the good news of the Gospel—of relating, love and forgiveness, of courage, discipline, and reaching out to others in real rather than bogus ways.

Psychoanalysis taught me to distinguish rain from sun, to be able more to tell the truth. It helped me see that my growing up had been far from easy and that trying to believe, while it had given me a community in which to grow, had also taught me to think everything would be wonderful if I tried harder to believe more! That experience of the gap between the words of theology and my life as I knew it taught me to beware any Gospel or words from the Church which imply we need nothing more than assent to those words to live a good and happy life. For me that whole idea had proved confusingly and frighteningly useless.

To be gay or lesbian necessarily sets us slightly apart. Our apartness may force us to forge links with other serious dancing partners in life—ecology, psychology, art, science, politics, community action, whatever we will (tap dancing if we like!) and to create other social spaces in which we belong. Dialogue brings Theology to life. Journey helps us see the shape of home. Standing apart may be useful.

The discovery of religious authority within the self

As the layers of what I had been unprepared to feel dropped away, I found that I desired both to live with my lesbian partner and to be ordained as a priest, all within a Church which didn't want to talk about being either a woman or gay, let alone both!

Luckily for me at that time another wise person befriended me. Monica Furlong, whom I met as Moderator of the Movement for the Ordination of Women, helped me to see that it was being lesbian which might prove useful in the oyster of my life as a priest. This awkward sand might eventually produce a pearl if I neither let it go nor escaped the oyster shell! What is that pearl? What treasure may gay and lesbian people have to discover and offer the Church?

The pearl is learning to individuate from the Church as institution and yet remain working within it as a free and healthy person calling other people to freedom and health. The grit in the oyster, never being completely "one" with the teaching of the Church, has allowed me to individuate from the Church to be my own person who is priest and woman and gay.

I arrive at tricky territory here in which to find a healthy place to stand.

What the Church of England *appears* to ask of its most successful priests is fusion between the priest's needs and those of the institution. In its "most successful" priests and ministers I frequently find people who assume that it is their calling to work all the time. I see people who are at the beck and call of the parish or diocese as if it were their own family. I see people who derive energy and purpose from the favour of a Father-Figure Bishop, in whom greater authority resides than within the self. I see many gay and lesbian leaders who feel unable to be "out".

Not that "being out" is a worthwhile goal for everyone. It is being *forced* not to be open which is damaging. The silencing of gay and lesbian priests is unhelpful because it does not allow us to explore, discover or speak from the position of our own spiritual authority, an authority wrought from our own dialogue between being captivated by Christ and gay. Silencing does not allow us to "grow up" within the Church. One result is a group of endlessly protesting Christians who appear caught in angry adolescent mode for ever. Another is a group of closet gay and lesbian Christians who appear unhealthily undifferentiated from the Church even while leading the lives of most bizarre sexual secrecy. I am struck by these words of the poet Michael Rosen, speaking once on "Desert Island Discs" because they relate to finding our own religious authority as much as to creating good art. "If you fib," he said, "the poem won't work".

Understanding the complexity of our human sexual identity

As Dean of Women in the Two Cities Area of the London Diocese I met regularly with other women and a small group of Bishops between 2002 and 2005 to talk about the development of the ministry of women as Bishops and Priests within the Church. Observing the conservatism of our leadership helped me understand just a little why we are still wed to biblical pictures of gender relations, family and community life, and sexual relationships—pictures from 2000-3000 years ago and from utterly different social milieus.

There has to be some strong reason to be so wed when the pictures given in the pages of the Bible are themselves so complex and changing over time that it becomes clear they cannot be used simply as a rule-book in sexual ethics.

There has to be some strong reason for maintaining so conservative a sexual ethic when our gifted and aware laypeople—parents and teachers, nurses and psychologists, counsellors and artists and biologists, know human life to be other for very many people than that which is described as ideal within statements from the Church regarding sexual ethics. Why, even our children and teenagers know that life is different in terms of sexual identity and the human journey towards maturity than is being openly spoken of in the Church.

There are so many problems springing from this lack of ability to talk openly about changes within our understanding of gender relations and sexual identity that it is hard to know where to start but I want to mention four which have affected me particularly as a priest and pastor.

Firstly—unless we assert that gay and lesbian people, whether alone or in committed relationships, are as capable of living a holy life as their heterosexual brother or sister we contribute to homophobia within our society. The child being bullied in the playground, the lesbian couple being stoned in the street for holding hands, the gay man struggling with whether it is possible to be a Christian and gay, do not hear the Church being open and welcoming. They hear the reiteration of what their family have probably already voiced— we love you but conditionally, you must change.

Secondly, unless we reach out to learn from the gay and lesbian community what it is like to be in their shoes we cannot begin to talk to the gay and lesbian world about sexual ethics, we cannot challenge the ethics of "the scene".

Thirdly, unless we permit gay and lesbian priests and Christian leaders to be open about their sexual orientation and relationships we do not create good role models for those who may be asking serious questions about themselves, especially the young and vulnerable, within our communities and congregations.

Fourthly, how can we maintain a high view of marriage, that in lifelong fidelity to the love of another who is different from us we glimpse something of the persistent and redeeming love of God, yet not bless gay and lesbian Christians committing themselves to one another? The advice not to bless gay and lesbian people willing to take the serious step in to Civil Partnership seems a cold withdrawal of generosity and support from those whose original family life may well place them most in need of both.

The parish priests, ministers and lay people of the Church, including its gay and lesbian members, are in a unique place of pastoral availability and stored wisdom to enter a discussion of the complexity of human sexuality in today's society and Church.

Creating spaces of integration and belonging

One of the joys in my life which helps me think it is worth it, trying to transform the world, and be myself transformed, is the existence of St Anne's Soho where I was the Rector from 1998-2007.

If you came to St Anne's you might wonder what on earth I am talking about. We look pretty normal most Sundays and in terms of numbers often quite fragile. But something is happening there to do with the transformation of the world—or at least that part of the world over which we have some agency: ourselves and our community and a small part of the wider world.

It is partly the result of our history. Though we are a tiny intense village we have to embrace diversity to manage to co-inhere together at all—on the school roll there are 130 children speaking 40 different languages. It is partly the result of the nature of our Church building. It was built 50 years after the Blitz destroyed the former Church, together with a thriving Community Centre all around it. We don't have to look for the community to come in to the Church—they are there already. It is more that we have to justify our usefulness to them, which is a challenging but fruitful way of life.

In this living with difference we experience the odd moment of romance and sentimentality but more usually we know great difficulty. The one who is very different from me creates the gap, the absence, the wound, showing me that diversity is not the byword for a comfortable life, but a real hard-edged place to be, of jarring and struggle and forgiveness, as we inch our way towards the wholeness in complexity for which we are made. We are learning to share the gift and burden of the rain, as are many churches quietly, painfully and joyfully. We are creating places of singing!

Singing in the Rain - a sharing of gifts

Gay and lesbian Christians carry the burden of understanding human sexual complexity from a very young age. They have learnt how to stand apart, to be both critical of the Gospel and the Church while listening and wanting to contribute. They have an authority stemming from an inner and outer wrestling with what it means to be both captivated by Christ and gay. Keenly aware of the need to belong, and able to recognise loneliness, they are capable of creating warm community for the welcome of others. When they fall in love for life the prejudice they have encountered renders them particularly aware of the miracle of long-term commitment and grateful for the grace of love. Like Pilgrims arriving at Pentecost we have much to say!

Clare Herbert

For discussion

I use pictures to give me space to see things in a new light so my questions involve drawing. If you hate drawing cut the crayons and go straight to the question.

o Draw your life as a line or road or tree. Place along it events and people who have helped form your ideas and your faith. What or who has been most influential in your creating your own view of faith and its role in your life?

o Draw your Church involvement and your interests outside Church as a series of separate and overlapping circles. Which circles act as Dancing Partners to your theology and your faith? Which offer most grounding and which most challenge?

o Imagine what life is like for a gay or lesbian Christian. Draw your fantasy of how they feel in relation to the Church. What safe spaces arise for gay and lesbian Christians in the Church and on the other hand what conflicts may they have in relation to their faith and life? (If you are gay or lesbian you may want to do this exercise for yourself or imagine instead a heterosexual person attempting to reconcile the journeys towards faith and sexual maturity)

For further reading

From a personal perspective:
James Alison, Faith beyond Resentment, Darton, Longman & Todd Ltd ISBN 0232524114

James Alison, On being Liked, Darton, Longman & Todd Ltd ISBN 023252517X

Monica Furlong, Bird of Paradise, Mowbray, ISBN 0264673360 , out of print but copies available via Amazon

Andrew Linzey and Richard Kirker ed., Gays and the Future of Anglicanism, O Books, ISBN 190504738

From a parish perspective
Jeffrey Heskins, Unheard Voices, DLT, 2001 ISBN 0232524270, again out of print but available via Amazon

From a global perspective
Terry Brown, Ed., Other Voices, Other Worlds, Darton, Longman & Todd, ISBN 525692

From a biblical perspective
Michael Vasey, Strangers and Friends, Hodder & Stoughton Religious, ISBN 0340608145

The LGCM website has a comprehensive list of book titles (see page 48)

Transforming Prayer
- Renewing Hope

Jim Cotter is an Anglican priest
who is currently priest in charge of
the parish of Aberdaron in North
Wales. He is one of the most
talented writers of Christian
prayers and his Cairns Publications
have provided a wealth of material
for worship and devotion.

Take the 'languages' of history, sexuality, psychotherapy, science, and law (etc.). Listen to languages other than one's mother tongue, either ancient or contemporary, Aramaic or Welsh (for example). Let them all converse with the inherited 'language' of Bible and Church and Theology. Make connections between them and let that connection inform the 'language' of liturgy. Then Christian corporate prayer might surge with hope. Mind and heart might no longer be split from each other, or even from body and imagination. We might recognize ourselves again, and one another, and the God of Jesus Christ who does not know how to love.

So much of the language regularly used in churches is cliché, true but worn out. I know that 'This is the Word of the Lord' can be understood more subtly than literally, but that is not, I think, how most people hear it. A question at the end of a reading, 'How is this the Word of the Lord for us today?', addressed to the preacher, might both sharpen the mind of the preacher and whet a congregation's appetite for a living word. It suggests a dialogue with the Bible rather than sitting under the Bible (or the pulpit, or the throne). It takes the work of the Holy Spirit seriously, making us expectant of a lively living word, chewable and memorable. An Australian cartoon depicts what looks like a bread delivery van, with the information on the side, 'Fresh words delivered daily' - or at least weekly.

It really is quite exhausting, spiritually depressing, to try and participate in an act of worship where the mind is constantly turning and twisting because the words being used no longer carry meaning for us. It is not that we think them untrue, nor do we wish to deny their value to those who first wrote and used them. But it is to recognize that so much of what we have inherited does not connect with heart and mind. It raises questions, and these are best explored in conversation and debate, rather than being given a supposed final answer from a pulpit. So, if we find ourselves internally arguing with much of what is said, we may retreat into inner silence, or slowly withdraw our energy and presence. There are many of our contemporaries who have done precisely that. It seems a pity if there is no alternative.

In particular, I am thinking of those parts of Scripture that portray an inhumane and subchristian God, a portrayal that has not passed through the lens of Jesus Christ. 'An eye for an eye' may have been an improvement on 'a life for an eye' but used in isolation continues to support revenge. To encourage love for one's neighbour may lessen the incidence of honour killings in the tribe, but still leaves plenty of room for being vicious to the next tribe. To proclaim that you cannot be a Christian unless you 'love your enemies' will notautomatically endear a preacher to a congregation, nor will the parable of the Good Samaritan, which at least implies that the wounded man (Jewish) had to let his enemy (Samaritan) love him.

I am thinking too of the ancient creeds, not least the Nicene, let alone the Athanasian. If members of congregations were asked to raise their hands at any line they did not believe or at least believed through different words, I suspect we would have a worse scene than at a chaotic auction. Living words lose their power when they become clichés. And creeds that were written to discourage and even exclude those who think outside the box perhaps deserve to become desiccated. I am thinking too of the 'language' of architecture, furnishings, choreography, and costume, so often in western Christianity reflecting the hierarchical and patriarchal assumptions and orders of manor house and monarch's court. At least the early rural Welsh churches were built on the model of the long barn of the farms, the gathering place for celebrations of the extended household - smaller, lower, and on one rather than three levels. Ask of any of these non-verbal 'languages', How do they speak of the character of

God? 'Petitions' and 'intercessions' are part of the royal patterning, the peasant hoping against hope that the king on rare progress through the realm might deign to stop and hear his plea and act on his behalf. 'I'll try anything in an emergency when I'm desperate. It probably won't work: after all the king has time for only a few petitions a day out of the hundred waving from the crowd. And anyway, God surely doesn't have time for the likes of me.' A far cry from the conviction that each and all are loved alike by God and nothing can stop that loving.

A more engaged and hopeful way of praying for others or for ourselves is to simply to hold the other or oneself to the heart of God, and breathing a blessing, all the time aware that we need to be prepared to act or change as part of the working out of that prayer. Try using 'Your kingdom come...Your will be done' rather than 'Lord, in your mercy...Hear our prayer.' And in a service the person 'leading' is not so much doing the praying as bidding everybody present to get down to it and do some spiritual work - even if it is simply the gift of one's time and stillness, asking not for something we have decided in advance would be to the other's good, but allowing our small contribution of energy to be aligned with God's, towards the greater well-being of the other. We are participating in the continuing creating and restoring power of God; we are renewed in the process; and hope is reborn. And the quieter the atmosphere the more expectant and hopeful we may become.

Religious debate still seems to be dominated by supporters and opponents of the old man on a throne in the sky. Even if we find the fathering activity of God a helpful picture, it is surprising that this image has so dominated Christian prayer, along with the status of lord and king, when the heart of a Christian understanding of God is trinitarian. The notion of 'trinity' is at least suggestive of dynamic relationship, of creative power, of an energy of love that flows between the one who is loving and the one who is receiving love. Addressing God as 'Life-giver, Pain-bearer, Love-maker' at least brings that possibility to mind - even if a passing flicker of recognition that 'love-maker' might affirm the sexual in our picturing of the divine is enough to make at least one liturgical commission of my acquaintance to substitute 'earth-maker', thus sparing the blushes of the synods.

Years ago, Paul Tillich wrote a book with the title Love, Power, and Justice, and much of the exploration of the language of prayer has to deal with those three great comprehensive words. How can each inform and influence the other (another trinitarian exercise)? Does the fact of the immense explosive energies at work in the universe still make us picture the Creator in similar - and even more violent - terms? A divine power that is greater than any other power? And is that the only way we can understand power at work in those who seek to live in the image of God as followers of Jesus? Deep waters indeed. Does justice imply retribution and revenge alone? Or at all? What price reconciliation and restoration? Which do we choose? Which is most deeply embedded in our minds and in our interpretations of the Bible? God as destructive, violent, explosive - sudden pressure - in a hurry - de-forming? Or God as creative, patient, persistent - gentle pressure, taking time - trans-forming? And does God go out at the head of our armies, bringing the heavenly 'hosts' to supplement our inferior numbers? It seems as if most followers of Jesus are hoping to be on the winning side at the final battle rather than at the side of their former enemy at the final banquet.

We are familiar with prayers that begin, 'Almighty God'. Now 'might' is most frequently associated with military force. The phrase in Welsh is 'Hollalluog Duw', with the root 'gallu' having some associations with overall ability rather than more narrowly, and almost entirely, with force (though today it includes that meaning). The power that is an energy and ability to get something done is akin to one of the Aramaic roots of 'Abba'. In both Welsh and Aramaic the meanings can be wider, deeper, and more creative than anything implied by the English word 'might'. Perhaps a prayer in English could begin, 'Living God, energetic and skilful in creating and restoring...'

To the objection that it is much longer than 'Almighty God...', well, of course it is, but perhaps our worship could do with being more leisurely, with periods of silence, and, overall, fewer words - but words that connect and nourish, with time to absorb them.

Or take the word 'mercy'. Is it poured upon us from on high, by one with the power to condemn or to free? Or is it embedded in a process of the telling of stories and the restoring of relationships? It is a word also associated with the exchange of 'merc'handise, at its best to the satisfaction of both customer and 'merc'hant, and evoking 'merc'i, thanks. And the process of forgiveness is perhaps best written with a series of hyphens: 'Forgive-us-ourtrespasses- as-we-forgive-those-who-trespass-against-us.' The human-human and the divinehuman are intertwined. The one flows into and out of the other. In the act of one person forgiving another the divine forgiveness is enacted in parable: the one partakes of the other.

Much of what I have written so far comes from reflection on the work of those scholars of history, Dominic Crossan and Marcus Borg, and I have touched on the language of law. To mention more briefly the languages of sexuality, psychotherapy, and science, I would simply give three illustrations of how bringing them to bear on the language of the psalms has resulted in fresh unfoldings of those ancient poems, as examples, a refrain for an unfolding of Psalm 144, and some verses from unfoldings of Psalms 63 and 104:

O Lover, divine and human,
intimate, insistent, and tender,
courteous in paying attention,
passionate in wholehearted embrace,
bring us alive and alight,
each a singular creation.

Refrain, An unfolding of Psalm 144

Courage have I found to face the creatures of the night,
the terrible faces masking cries of abandonment,
swords that glint in the darkness protecting the weak,
jackals that swoop on those who dare near.
The faces of terror will prove my friends yet,
guarding as they do my fragile soul-self,
waiting the calm word of the approach of true love,
wanting to be named as faithful and true.
So I shall emerge to the place of rejoicing,
the child and the adult linked arm in arm.
We shall see your face in all your creatures,
we shall know the truth in our hearts.

An unfolding of part of Psalm 63

Light from the dawn of the cosmos,
reaching out over billions of years;
the sun so familiar and steady,
spun off from that ancient fireball.
the primal explosion murmurs,
we hear the hiss of the aeons,
whispering insistent relic
of the original moment of time.

The beginning was all flame,
and the flame was unfurled into time;
all that has come into being
began at the heart of the flame.

Slowly the fire cooled,
the storm of particles ceased,
combed into structures of matter,
clouds and clusters of galaxies.

The cosmic dust was scattered –
a heart bursting into stars:
truly strange is our ancestor –
we ride on its pulsing still.

Refrain
Marvellous and vigorous,
splendidly unfolding,
the wonders of creation
we contemplate with awe.
Praise be to the Creator:
fresh energy divine
with passion and with tenderness
brings beauty new to birth.

Part of an unfolding of Psalm 104

Finally, there is one psalm that perhaps focuses most of what I have been trying to express in this brief survey of possible ways of using language through dialogue of ancient and modern to reinvigorate our prayer and worship and make us more hopeful.

Psalm 58 is full of anger and is usually avoided in public worship. But anger, clearly acknowledged, is near neighbour to compassion. And the deeper the anger, the more that, transformed, it can be channelled in compassionate action. In unfolding the psalm I have if anything made the anger even more virulent than in the original, using phrases like 'break their teeth,' 'shatter their jaws', 'let them be trodden down and wither like grass,' 'let them be cut down like thorns before they know it,' 'the just shall rejoice when they see your vengeance.' Prayer begins with honesty about our stories and our feelings, and about what in such moods we would relish God doing: but it doesn't stop there, self-satisfied and selfrighteous.

Here are the last three verses of the psalm:

Have mercy upon us, have mercy,
criminals and judges with the roughest of justice.
No plea can we enter before you.
It is the deprived and homeless, ragged and shivering,
who stand in the court to accuse us.

Those on the edge, unkempt, unacceptable,
they are the ones who show us your face.
And, deep within, is a child who is shunned,
whom we treat as our enemy, battered and bruised.

O when will we learn to stretch out our arms,
to receive from the outcasts and scapegoats
the redeeming embrace and the melting of tears:
in them and them only is our last dying hope.

And the refrain is this:

The faces of the downtrodden accuse us:
only the destitute can redeem.

None of that is easy or comfortable. To see clearly and to be involved personally in the praying will not make us optimistic, but it may make us hopeful. To be optimistic is to expect everything to be all right without our needing to change, to be hopeful is to be changed in the midst of that which is not yet right, but expectant of surprise.

Jim Cotter

For reflection and discussion

o Consider the words used in worship. How can they best retain their power and meaning for today's worshippers? Share examples with others of prayers/hymns/etc which hold meaning for you and those which do not.

o Should ancient creedal statements be used in worship and is there a place for other affirmations? As an exercise, members of the group could be asked to write their own personal creed.

o Jim Cotter writes of a more hopeful way of praying. How would you describe your understanding and practice of prayer?

o What are the most helpful images of God for you in worship?

For further reading

Jim Cotter has written extensively, offering compilations of psalms, prayers, resources for different liturgies etc. The easiest way to see this range of resources is to visit www.cottercairns.co.uk. There are also downloadable resources.

There is an abundance of books on prayer but those which specifically offer resource material for worship and personal devotion include:

Janet Morley, All Desires Known, SPCK Publishing ISBN 0281056889

Janet Morley, Praying with the World's Poor, SPCK Publishing ISBN 0281056986

Geoffrey Duncan has edited various excellent collections of prayers, readings etc, most of which can be found as titles published by SCM Canterbury Press.

Hannah Ward and Jennifer Wild have compiled resources for worship which follow the lectionary readings, published over three titles by Westminster/John Knox Press, U.S.

Wild Goose Publications have excellent compilations of resource material (see page 56)

Jonny Baker and Doug Gay, Alternative Worship, SPCK Publishing ISBN 0281053960

Richard Giles, Creating Uncommon Worship, Canterbury Press ISBN 9781853115905

Dilly Baker, A Place at the Table, Canterbury Press, ISBN 9781853117725

Steven Shakespeare, Prayers for an Inclusive Church, to be published in September 2008 by Canterbury Press. An important new resource of liturgical material to be used in Common Worship over the three year cycle

Browsing the web will also produce a wealth of liturgical material as will visiting the websites of liturgical publishers.

Resourcing from the Web

As with every aspect of life, the web offers endless ideas and resources for those on the religious quest. As the number of well stocked theological/religious booksellers declines, so we are reliant more and more on the websites of publishers to browse through their catalogues on line. Some publishing houses try their best to give reasonable descriptions of the books on offer but of course this is second best to a good browse in a bookshop! Websites abound to promote all kinds of religious groups and organisations and through their various links, a whole network of sites can be visited. Churches increasingly are putting liturgical and other resources on to their websites, as are national and regional denominational bodies.

Listed below are just a few of the websites which you may find useful.

a) Publishing houses

www.scm-canterburypress.co.uk
www.spck.org.uk
www.darton-longman-todd.co.uk
www.obooks.com
www.hodder.co.uk
www.oneworld-publications.com
www.harpercollins.com
www.chpublishing.co.uk
www.westarinstitute.org
www.continuumbooks.com

b) Learning resources

Increasingly but not plentifully there can be found various courses for individuals, groups, churches to access.

www.livingthequestions.com

Living the Questions is a USA product featuring many of the writers in the progressive theological world. The course is DVD based with downloadable resources (see page 50).

www.foundations21.org.uk

The Bible Reading Fellowship offers this web based discipleship course, which is described as covering Christian basics. For many the content may not break much radical new ground but others will find its colourful imagery and contemporary approach appealing.

www.beta-course.org.uk

Written and presented by Dr Sara Savage, Rev Dr Fraser Watts and Ruth Layzell from the Psychology and Christianity Project at the University of Cambridge, this 10 session course is decidedly pastoral and therapeutic with an emphasis placed on the importance of relationships and the need for healing and wholeness in ourselves and in our relationships. For some people it might be a good alternative to Alpha.

c) Other resources

www.johnshelbyspong.com

Bishop Jack Spong has had an extraordinary ministry in the Anglican church. Over many years he has challenged the church to see that nothing less than a wholesale re-visioning of Christianity will fit it for the twenty first century. In addition to his many books, you can subscribe to his online weekly essay.

www.ekklesia.co.uk

Describing itself as a think-tank that promotes transformative theological ideas in public life, this site has a wealth of news and views, columns and features.

www.shipoffools.com

The ship of fools website offers through its mystery worshipper a somewhat colourful but useful view of scores of churches up and down the country. If you want to know what to expect from Church X it's worth browsing the Ship of Fools archives!

www.radicalfaith.org

An interesting site for liberal Christians, coming from The Society of the Sacred Mission, with sermons, book reviews and other features.

www.christian.net

This website describes itself as an online Christian community and does contain a great deal of resource material.

www.affirmingcatholicism.org.uk

Affirming Catholicism describes itself as a movement of inspiration and hope in the Anglican Communion, seeking to bring together and strengthen lay and ordained people who recognize the positive, inclusive and joyful currents in the Catholic tradition of Christianity.

www.ccc4vat2.co.uk

This unusual website name actually stands for Catholics for a Changing Church, whose patron is Hans Küng. The site has a number of essays, reviews etc by those who are definitely on the liberal wing of the Roman Catholic community.

www.sofn.org.uk

The Sea of Faith network has as its strapline "Exploring and promoting religious faith as a human creation..." This is a site worth visiting to understand more clearly the views of those often on the edge of our church communities.

www.beliefnet.com

This American site describes itself as being independent of any one religious tradition and indeed has a huge resource bank covering different faith traditions.